"... the foreworder"
R. H. Dillon

Night Landing

A Short History of West Coast Smuggling

David W. Heron

Illustrations by Kirk Peterson

CENTRAL POINT, OREGON

Night Landing

Published by Hellgate Press, an imprint of PSI Research, Inc.
Copyright 1998 by David W. Heron

For information or to direct comments, questions, or suggestions regarding this book and other Hellgate Press books, contact:

    Editorial Department
    Hellgate Press
    P.O. Box 3727
    Central Point, OR 97502

    (541) 479-9464 *telephone*
    (541) 476-1479 *fax*
    info@psi-research.com *e-mail*

Editor: Janelle Davidson
Book designer: Constance C. Dickinson
Compositor: Jan O. Olsson
Illustrator: Kirk Peterson
Cover designer: Steven Burns

Heron, David W. (David Winston), 1920–
    Night Landing : a short history of West Coast smuggling / David W. Heron.
        p. cm.
    Includes index.
    ISBN (invalid) 1-55571-449-8 (pbk.)
    1. Smuggling—California—History.   I. Title.
HJ6690.H47 1998
364.1'33—dc21
                                       98-50889

Printed and bound in the United States of America
First edition 10 9 8 7 6 5 4 3 2 1

 Printed on recycled paper when available.

Contents

Foreword

The subtitle of David Heron's book on a neglected subject of California's socio-economic history is accurate enough — to a point. The volume is, indeed, a short history of smuggling on the West Coast, and an interesting one, to boot.

But it is more than that, for in documenting the changes that have gone on in smuggling over the years, the text shifts away from an anecdotal account of the romanticized smuggling of California's Spanish and Mexican days to the facts of a bleaker present.

The secret introduction of New England trade goods to rancheros in order to evade Spanish laws and Mexican customs duties, like the concomitant sneaking out of sea otter skins by William Shaler and other *Yanquis* to thwart a Spanish monopoly on this fur trade, was not only tolerated by California's citizenry, including many minor officials, but was cheered. And it is applauded by us today.

We admired the ingenuity of these *contrabandistas* because, in a sense, they democratized a far-off province subject to autocratic rule from Madrid and Mexico City. And, importantly, this form of smuggling was victimless.

During the subsequent American period till well after World War I, activity in this area of illicit trade ran from individual travellers cheating on taxes (with hidden jewelry purchases) to less-tolerable gun running, opium smuggling, and the importation of illegals, Chinese by sea and Mexicans across the desert border.

The one big post-war business was bootlegging. Unlike the case in Al Capone's Chicago, coastal California remained relatively peaceful during the traumatic period of Prohibition. I used to play aboard a captured rum runner, tied to a Sausalito dock, when I was a kid during the Depression. I remember well that bootleggers, including those jailed for their sins, were looked upon more as heroes than criminals, and were certainly not seen as villains in any sense. They were simply considered to be men who had run afoul of a bad law in order to right a wrong — Prohibition.

But as Heron shows us, by mixing what we used to call Current Events with earlier and more traditional history and adding a bit of investigative reporting, traditional smuggling has become degraded since World War II. There is nothing romantic about the disgraceful cartels that have replaced relatively benign contraband with such destructive, deadly drugs as cocaine and heroin. Misery has replaced adventure. International violence and, above all, *greed* (the latter enormous, astonishing, measured in billions, not millions, of dollars) have replaced the cunning of customs-dodging rugged individuals.

So, be warned! What starts out as a colorful antiquarian story ends up as a cautionary tale for all of us.

RICHARD H. DILLON

Author, historian, and former director of the Sutro Library, San Francisco

Preface

The venerable *Oxford English Dictionary (OED)* says the word *smuggle* was used in the late seventeenth century and that it is a cousin of the Low German *smukkeln*, Dutch *smokkeln*, Danish *smugle*, and Norwegian *smugla*, all of which, says the *OED*, have to do with conveying "goods clandestinely into or out of a country or district, in order to avoid payment of legal duties, or in contravention of some enactment . . . ."

The smugglers whose adventures you will read about in the pages which follow were most of them unaware that they were practitioners of an ancient profession — not the oldest, of course, but certainly one of the more mature. And as long as we have customs duties, immigration quotas, and wars on drugs, the profession continues. Today's news is all too full of the flood tide of cocaine from the northwestern highlands of South America and the rusty ships full of hopeful Fujianese lured into brutal indenture by tales of great wealth.

In gathering these stories I have been generously assisted by the Bancroft Library in Berkeley, particularly by Walter Brem; by the National Archives and Records Service branch in San Bruno, especially by William Greene; by Irene Stachura of the J. Porter Shaw Library of the San Francisco Maritime National Historical Park; by the staff of the McHenry Library of the University of California at Santa Cruz, particularly by Margaret Gordon, Stanley Stevens, Carol Champion, Paul Stubbs, Joanne Nelson, and Maureen Lucas; by Patricia Pfremmer, Santa Cruz County Law Librarian; and by the U.S. Coast Guard Group, Monterey, particularly CWO Craig Bitler.

I am indebted to Richard Dillon not only for his gracious foreword but also for careful reading of the manuscript and correction of a number of small but crucial flaws, and to Janelle Davidson for her patient and perceptive editing, to Phil Reader for revealing a handful of indispensable Prohibition figures, to Bill Pickelhaupt for his whitehall boat lore, and to Steve Lawton, CEO and artistic director of Otter B Books, for advice and encouragement.

And finally to my wife Winifred, gentle critic and eagle-eyed copy editor, patient with the clutter of books and papers piled high around the tube in a corner of her pleasant and otherwise businesslike studio.

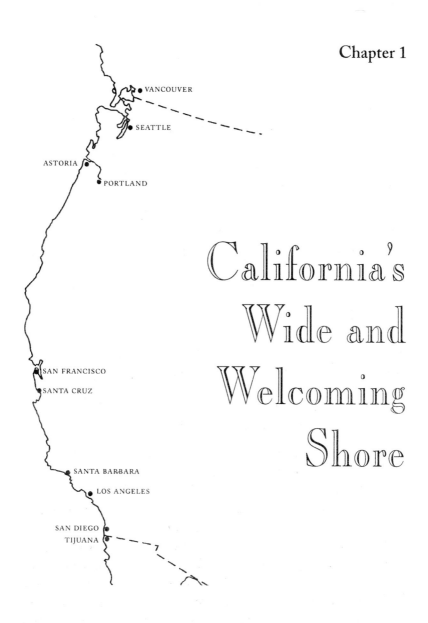

Chapter 1

California's Wide and Welcoming Shore

The lure of smuggling is as old as frontiers, as taxation, as a tinker's trek from one fiefdom to the next. The covert carrying across a border of something either prohibited or seen as prohibitively taxed pervades our history, and the West Coast's record is in some ways outstanding.

The bays and beaches of California have a rich history of nocturnal traffic in contraband. Although in recent years much of California's smuggling has been by air and across the Mexican border, over the years the Pacific Ocean has been the dominant contraband trade route.

The list of contraband is endlessly varied. The most common these days are narcotics, watches, jewelry, orchids, alcohol, and people. But fashions change. In thirteenth century England, the contraband was wool, exported across the channel to France. Eighteenth century American colonists were accused of evading British trade laws and of selling supplies to the enemy during the French and Indian War.

In the early years of the nineteenth century Yankee traders like Captain George Washington Eayrs brought silks from the Orient and finery from Europe to Californians, isolated by Spanish prohibitions and an overextended supply line from Mexico City, in exchange for otter pelts, much prized in the Orient.

Several decades later, Chinese immigrants followed their relatives, recruited to build the transcontinental railroads. Then, frustrated by the xenophobia which produced the Chinese Exclusion Act of 1882, they occasionally avoided long periods of detention at Customs by covert landing at night. In the same Victorian era a taste for opium, fostered in China by the British East India Company, followed the Chinese to San Francisco and the gold fields. In June 1848, Congress passed a law prohibiting "the importation of adulterated and spurious drugs and medicines," which promptly became a challenge to smugglers. Toward the end of the century opium was the contraband drug of choice. Although its import was not initially prohibited, stiff import duties were the incentive.[1]

With the turn of the century began a period in which the Coast Guard was able to devote more time to maritime safety and the

Customs Service to minor evasions of import duties. This ended, however, with the Eighteenth Amendment and the Volstead Act enforcing the prohibition against liquor. The Prohibition Era, from its beginning in 1920 to repeal in 1933, is credited by several scholars as the principal source of today's organized crime. Certainly, for thirteen years, rumrunning was a major American industry, and it flourished on the Pacific coast.[2]

Smuggling was less conspicuous during the late 1930s, World War II, and even the Cold War period, when customs inspectors were again able to concentrate on small consignments of Swiss watches, expensive perfume, and jewelry, the latter of which brought some well-known people into the smuggling spotlight. During the 1960s, however, the international drug trade was developing, and it has increasingly dominated the smuggling industry up to the present time. Its billion-dollar profits and pervasive corruption have in some ways eclipsed even the most spectacular crimes of the Prohibition era.

Yet fashions continue to change. *The New York Times* reported in May 1995 that, at that time, the commodity second only to drugs as the national favorite for smugglers was freon, a chlorofluorocarbon which had been used almost universally as a refrigerant until it was discovered that it was destroying the atmosphere's ozone layer.[3] The United States had joined 139 other nations in signing the Montreal Protocol in 1987, pledged to finding safer substitutes for freon. However, since freon has for years been used in most refrigerators and auto air conditioners and since most acceptable substitutes require expensive equipment modification, the change has been gradual. The United States, instead of banning existing stocks, charges $5.35 per pound on all sales of the gas. This is an incentive to find substitutes, but it has also generated large stocks of black-market freon, smuggled from abroad or produced without federal quality control and sold without payment of the $5.35 a pound in federal taxes.[4]

Other recent and exotic contraband in the shipping news includes plutonium and zirconium, both used in nuclear bombs and abundantly stockpiled in Russia, where they appear to be slipping through the international efforts at containment; counterfeit holograms made in Shanghai for bootlegged Microsoft products; counterfeit Levi's, also from China; rare and endangered orchids from southeast Asia; and parts of endangered animals, such as a Siberian tiger skeleton, dried bear bile, and rhinoceros horn.[5]

Although cocaine, marijuana, and heroin have been the contraband of choice in the final decades of the twentieth century, the traffic in illegal immigrants has recently contributed its share to public anxiety, to the xenophobia which in 1995 produced anti-immigration laws in California, and to reinforcement of the Immigration and Naturalization Service along the Mexican border.

The Pacific Coast's two centuries of smuggling owe less to laws and government efforts at enforcement than to frontier traditions of personal freedom, the gold rush, the self-reliance of the Old West, and the streak of prickly paranoid anarchy which has recently surfaced in the private militia movement. As a result, smugglers have suffered much less public disapproval than have robbers, rapists, and murderers.

Epitomizing the era of acceptance, *San Francisco Chronicle* columnist Helen Dare asserted in 1911 that women were more assiduous smugglers than men but complained that customs inspectors were becoming intolerable. She said:

> Really, what's the use of going abroad any more if you can't get anything in? Where's the pleasure of getting home, and unpacking, and meeting your curious, admiring, interested friends, who naturally expect to see something — and to get something — if in the safe seclusion behind your own door you can't astonish them with the contraband treasures, the loot that you "brought in?"[6]

Why is smuggling generally less despised than other crimes? Certainly the effects of the drug trade are horrific, as are the modern slave ships of Taiwan. Still, the lament of tourist Helen Dare has its appeal. In the halcyon days before eagle-eyed customs inspectors, smuggling was not a violent crime, and though smuggling is not without victims, many of its ill effects are inconspicuous, if not invisible.

Invisibility is an important condition for successful smuggling. If the importers' wares are compact and ingeniously concealed, the smugglers' arrival can be forthright. If weight or volume are significant, night landing in the solitude of a deserted beach is preferred, although sometimes complicated. If concealment is impossible, investment in friendly discretion is one of the costs of doing business. Bribery is significant in the cocaine trade but may have been even more pervasive during Prohibition.

Despite the public's leniency toward smugglers, their crimes have been serious in the eyes of the law, and as a rule when they have been caught they have lost their newfound wealth and gone to prison. Such was the fate of Captain Eayrs, who evaded the Spanish laws against foreign commerce early in the nineteenth century and brought camel-hair shawls, fishhooks, crockery, and candy to California missionaries and ranchers' wives.

Spanish authorities imprisoned him in 1813 and confiscated his cargo. A kindred victim of underestimating the Establishment was Calvin Robinson, whose first cargo of hashish and marijuana in 1986 sold like hotcakes along the Sacramento River delta but whose second, bigger and better, the following year, was lost and cost him a life sentence in the federal penitentiary.

Although the rewards of successful smuggling have often been generous, a little bad luck has occasionally resulted in miserable failure. The stories which follow have been revealed, as a rule, when smugglers' caution, luck, or ingenuity ran out. Thus reports of their escapades have come primarily through court trial records and news reporters' accounts. We shall never know how many shadowy West Coast entrepreneurs, proceeding cautiously and patiently, resisting the temptation to overexpand, have made a comfortable living smuggling dope, jewelry, pirated software, or indentured workers into California and other western states.

"Not many people are scrupulous about smuggling," wrote Adam Smith, father of political economy, in 1776, "when, without perjury, they can find any easy and safe opportunity of doing so . . . ."[7]

Endnotes

1. William M. Clements Library, *Eighteenth Century Documents Relating to the Royal Forests, the Sheriffs and Smuggling; Selected from the Shelbourne Manuscripts*, ed. Arthur Lyon Cross (New York: Macmillan, 1928), pp. 21–23; and Carl E. Prince, and Mollie Keller, *The United States Customs Service: a Bicentennial History* (Washington: Government Printing Office, 1989), pp. 221–222.

2. *Law, Alcohol, and Order: Perspectives on National Prohibition*, Contributions in American History, ed. David E. Kyvig, no. 110 (Westport, CT: Greenwood Press, 1985); Andrew Sinclair, *Prohibition: the Era of Excess* (Boston: Little, Brown & Co., 1962); and Everett S. Allen, *The Black Ships: Rumrunners of Prohibition* (Boston: Little, Brown & Co., 1979).

3. *The New York Times* 1 May 1995, p. 1 ff.

4. *San Francisco Chronicle* 17 August 1995, sec. C, p. 1.

5. *San Francisco Chronicle* 12 August 1994, sec. D, p. 6; 29 August 1994, sec. A, p. 19; 22 April 1995, sec. D, p. 1; 5 April 1995, sec. A, p. 22; and *San Jose Mercury News* 16 August 1994, sec. A, p. 7.

6. *San Francisco Chronicle* 18 January 1911, p. 7.

7. Adam Smith, *An Inquiry into the Nature and Causes of the Wealth of Nations* (Oxford: The Clarendon Press, 1976), 2: 898.

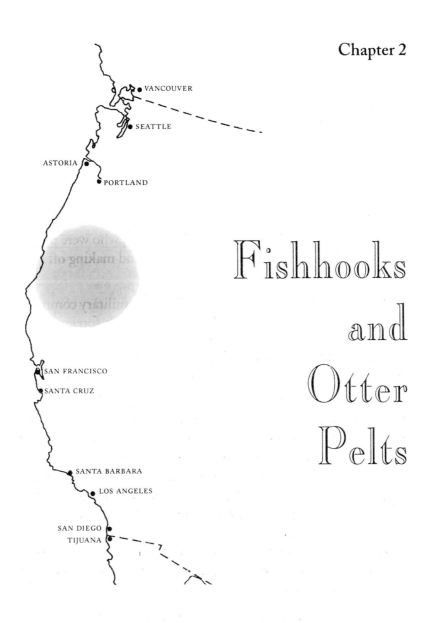

Chapter 2

Fishhooks and Otter Pelts

In 1806, when José Joaquín de Arrillaga returned to Monterey as governor of Alta California, the province was peaceful and the missions and cattle ranches were flourishing. But Arrillaga had one curious source of anxiety and frustration. Sea otters.

Arrillaga had already been governor twice, first from 1793 to 1794 then from 1800 to 1804, when in late 1805 he received a regular appointment signed by Charles IV. His next fifteen years in office set an all-time record for tenure as chief executive of California.[1] While he presided over a simpler enterprise than that of his recent successors, yet he faced a serious problem. His small and loose-knit military establishment left most of the coast defenseless against the rising tide of foreigners, who were prowling this rich and beautiful Spanish outpost and making off with its bounty.

In early February 1806, Arrillaga ordered the military commanders of California to prevent any commerce with foreign ships, to establish a strict guard on shore whenever a foreign ship entered a harbor, to confine all residents to their homes as long as the ship remained, and to report any foreign incursion promptly to the nearest presidio (a military-fortified settlement).[2]

Illegal immigration was not a serious concern; it was nearly half a century later that immigrants began to pose a real threat. It was casual visitors, foreign naval ships, and New England merchantmen which worried Spanish administrators. Appearance on the California coast of the Count de la Perouse in 1785 and of George Vancouver in 1792, as well as of the Russian vessel *Juno* in 1805 all served to remind the Spanish governor of how thinly the long coastline was defended. Particularly troublesome were the port commanders' experiences with merchant ships from New England.

American merchant seamen visited, and were drawn to, the California coast well before 1800. Since 1776, when members of Captain Cook's *Endeavor* crew had brought home reports that the pelts of sea otters were highly valued in China, otter hunting had become a growing industry on the western coast of North America, from the Aleutian Islands in Alaska to the Channel

Islands near Santa Barbara in California. This was why sea otters were the new focus of attention for Governor Arrillaga.

A preeminent nineteenth century marine biologist, C. M. Scammon, described sea otters as "the most valuable fur-bearing animals inhabiting the waters of the northwest coast of North America." He went on to describe them in detail.

> "The length of the full-grown animal may average five feet, including the tail, which is about ten inches. The head resembles that of the fur seal, having full, black, piercing eyes, exhibiting much intelligence .... The fur is of a much lighter shade inside than on the surface, and extending over all are scattering long glistening hairs, which add much to the richness and beauty of the pelage .... The ears are less than an inch in length, quite pointed, standing nearly erect, and are covered with short hair .... Sea-otter hunters along the coasts of California and Oregon were made up from nearly all the maritime nations of Europe and America, as well as from the different tribes of natives that dwelt near the sea-shore." [3]

A Sea Otter

As otter pelts increased Californians' purchasing power, the demand for imported goods grew apace. However, priests in the missions and soldiers in the presidios were chronically disappointed with the quantity and quality of the goods on Spanish ships which came up from San Blas, Mexico. New England merchants promptly recognized this sparsely populated and virtually undefended coast as a lucrative market.[4]

Among the best known and most interesting accounts of New Englanders' arrival on the west coast is that of the *Lelia Byrd*, in March 1803, and of the adventures of Bostonians Captain William Shaler and his partner and first officer, Richard Cleveland, in their efforts, generally successful, to evade the Spaniards' prohibitions against foreign commerce in California.[5] According to historian H. H. Bancroft in his seven-volume *The History of California*, the *Lelia Byrd* sailed for California in November 1801, "loaded with a great variety of merchandise which it was hoped to sell profitably on the west coast of America, no matter how, when, or where."[6]

After the long hard trip around Cape Horn, the Americans stopped in July 1802 for repairs in San Blas, where they sold a substantial part of their cargo, bought supplies, and eventually acquired 1,600 California otter pelts. The *Lelia Byrd* arrived in San Diego on March 16, 1803, and entered the harbor without incident. The next day Commandant Manuel Rodríguez, with an armed escort of twelve men, came aboard to ascertain what supplies the ship needed and to order its prompt departure. Rodríguez gave the crew permission to land but left his sergeant and five men aboard as a guard.

Cleveland later complained that Rodríguez was pompous, but early in their stay he discovered from the sergeant that the commandant had a thousand otter pelts in his warehouse. Part of this collection Rodríguez had confiscated from another New Englander, Captain John Brown of the *Alexander*, who had done some business in the harbor earlier in the month.

After his success in San Blas, Cleveland was convinced that Rodríguez would sell him the skins, but the commandant refused, and having delivered their supplies, he came aboard on March 21 to collect payment for them and to wish him and Shaler a pleasant voyage, suggesting that it was time for the *Lelia Byrd* to depart San Diego.

Richard J. Cleveland

That night, to avoid leaving San Diego empty-handed, Cleveland recalled:

> We sent the small boat ashore and purchased twenty-five skins of the soldiers, which we brought on board between eight and nine p.m. Having agreed for another lot, which were to be brought down to the shore abreast the vessel, we sent the longboat for them, with the first officer and two men. They did not return; and next morning, seeing the boat hauled up and our men, apparently guarded by soldiers, I went ashore with four hands, armed with pistols, and brought them off, together with the longboat.[7]

When he went ashore, Cleveland had also, apparently, taken with him one member of the sergeant's guard who escaped while the prisoners were being untied and hurried to the fort to tell the corporal in command that the ship was about to sail without releasing the other guards. As the *Byrd* approached the fort, the corporal fired a blank charge, to no effect, and then fired a nine-pound ball across the bow, several more which damaged the rigging, and one which made "an ugly hole between wind and water."[8]

The wind was light, and the ship made slow progress against a flood tide, but "as soon as we were abreast the fort we opened upon them," Cleveland recalled, "and in ten minutes silenced their battery and drove everyone out of it." As soon as the ship was out of range of the battery, the apprehensive sergeant and his men were put ashore.

Two days later the *Byrd* arrived in San Quintín, down the west coast of Baja California, there found Captain John Brown and the *Alexander*, and spent two months repairing hull and rigging in preparation for a trip across the Pacific. In late May the *Byrd* sailed for Hawaii and then China, where Cleveland sold the pelts at a good profit.

The Brigantine *Alert*

Cleveland then returned to Boston, aboard the *Alert*, with a cargo of silk, but Shaler sailed back to the west coast, getting as far north as the mouth of the Columbia River. Remembering past difficulties in San Diego, he stayed away from the presidios, landed first at Trinidad Bay, 300 miles north of San Francisco, where he acquired some otter pelts, then made his way south, avoiding major ports, and later reported, "I got abundant supplies of provisions and began trade with the missionaries and inhabitants for furs."[9]

Entering the California fur scene later that year, 1803, was an energetic young Irishman named Joseph O'Cain. O'Cain had sailed as first mate on the *Enterprise* in 1801, and in October 1803, he arrived on the Pacific coast in command of his own 280-ton ship, the *O'Cain*, which belonged to the Winship family of Boston, with Jonathan Winship, Jr. aboard. When O'Cain arrived on Kodiak Island, he suggested to Alexander Baranov, governor of the Russian outpost, an otter-hunting partnership.

An Aleutian Baidarka

O'Cain's plan was simple. Since trading with the Spanish was so difficult and uncertain, the Russians would recruit skillful Aleut hunters, who, with their *baidarkas* (kayaks) would travel aboard the *O'Cain* to islands off the coast of California where they could hunt the abundant otters without Spanish interference. Americans and Russians would divide the skins equally and greatly enhance their profits by eliminating the intermediary dealings with the Spanish.

Alexander A. Baranov, Governor of Kodiak Island

Baranov was somewhat hesitant to enter a partnership with a foreign interloper in what he regarded as Russian waters, but with insufficient resources of his own to make an effective Russian presence along the rich coast to the south, he saw promise in O'Cain's proposal, and accepted his contract. As surety, O'Cain left merchandise worth 12,000 rubles with Baranov on Kodiak. This partnership would flourish for almost a decade and eventually lead to the near extinction of the furry little mammals on the coast of California.

In less than two months the *O'Cain* was off the San Diego coast, and in mid-December it arrived in San Quintín, where in response to a heartrending hard-luck story Commandant José Manuel Ruíz gave permission to stay for a few days. Aboard the *O'Cain* were forty Aleut hunters and twenty baidarkas, which gave Ruíz good reason for apprehension.

The *O'Cain* was still there in early March 1804, in spite of frequent and emphatic orders to depart. It was then, almost three months after the ship's arrival, that Governor Arrillaga reported in frustration to the viceroy that "there is not an otter left from Mission Rosario to Santo Domingo." When O'Cain returned to Kodiak, he turned over half of his 1,100 skins to Baranov. He had acquired 700 additional skins, which he did not divide, by quiet trading with the Spaniards.[10]

In early 1806 the Boston fleet was back on the Pacific coast. Jonathan Winship took command of the *O'Cain* and Joseph O'Cain of the *Eclipse*. Both contracted with Baranov to bring him pelts in exchange for his providing and equipping Aleut hunters. Another Bostonian, Oliver Kimball, aboard the *Peacock*, soon joined the fleet, depositing Aleut hunters on islands off the lower California coast. For the most part they avoided confrontation with the Spanish authorities.

Captain O'Cain, however, was an assertive Irishman and indulged in one direct challenge to the Spaniards. Kimball was O'Cain's brother-in-law, and when O'Cain learned that the pilot of the *Peacock* had been captured north of San Diego, he reciprocated by capturing Corporal Juan Osuna and his men at Todos Santos, on the coast south of San Diego. When he released Osuna he instructed him to tell Commandant Rodríguez that he planned to blow up the San Diego fortifications. The *Eclipse's* eighteen guns were capable of doing the San Diego battery considerable damage, but O'Cain apparently decided not to risk the attack. Shortly thereafter, five of his men were captured when their longboat was wrecked near San José del Cabo.[11]

As Russian commander in the north Pacific, Baranov was painfully aware that the otter hunting would be more profitable if he did not have to split the proceeds with the Yankee traders. In 1809 the Russians established a base at Bodega Bay, north of

15

San Francisco, and three years later built a fort above it, which they named Rossiya (Russia), soon known as Fort Ross, and sent their Aleutian hunters down the coast and into San Francisco Bay. Their numbers eventually alarmed the Spanish, who captured as many hunters as they could.

Fort Ross, Kodiak Island

To avoid the guns of the presidio, the Aleuts landed north of the Golden Gate (the strait connecting San Francisco Bay with the Pacific Ocean) and carried their canoes across the peninsula to the North Bay, where for some time they were able to take otters with impunity. In late March of 1809, twenty canoes landed south of the mission settlement, and a Spanish patrol killed four hunters and wounded two, who were captured before the rest fled.[12]

There were some traders who experienced more success in their efforts. One of the more successful American captains was George Washington Eayrs. Eayrs was supercargo (an officer in a merchant ship in charge of the commercial concerns of the voyage) on William Heath Davis's *Mercury* and had gathered over 2,800 pelts during 1806 and 1807, most of them by trading with Spaniards. In the spring of 1808, Eayrs contracted with Baranov to carry Aleut hunters to the California coast, and by mid-summer of 1809 he left with over 2,000 skins. In the fall of that year he was back, both hunting and bartering.

For four years Eayrs maintained a cordial relationship with the California mission communities, supplying them with camel-hair shawls, English blankets, Chinese silk, fishhooks, gun-powder, hardware, crockery, and sugar candy in exchange for otter pelts, candles, meat, flour, and fresh produce.[13] In the summer of 1813, however, he was captured by Captain Nicolás Noé of the Spanish merchant vessel *Flora*, who said he did it because the American smugglers' prices kept him from selling his cargo in Monterey. Eayrs never recovered his ship and was held captive for over two years.[14]

Though the Russians were still contracting with the New Englanders, Baranov had been planning for some time to operate without them. As early as 1808 Ivan Kuskov, aboard the *Kodiak*, was in Bodega Bay, returning to Sitka in August 1809 with over 2,000 skins; in 1811 and 1812 he was back, aboard the *Chirikov*.

Because it was a time of uncertainty for both the Catholic Church in Spain and for the Spanish monarchy, pressed by Napoleon and by the people clamoring for governmental reform, Spanish supply ships from San Blas were slow to arrive and their cargoes were disappointing. Arrillaga was forced to admit, in reporting to Viceroy Calleja in 1819, that privation had forced him to condone open commerce with both the Yankee traders and the Russians.[15]

On the other hand the Spanish learned from their frequent contact with the foreigners that even without ships they could discourage the smugglers and otter hunters. In 1815 José de la Guerra y Noriega, military commander at Santa Barbara, captured seven members of the *Ilmen* crew at Refugio, where they had landed to rustle some cattle. The captain escaped only by swimming through the surf, but the supercargo and the Russian commander of the hunters were captured and taken to Mexico before they were finally released.[16]

Spanish defenses against smuggling were deteriorating, however. The padres were increasingly forthright in their overtures to such merchant traders as Eliab Grimes, captain of the *Eagle*, who in 1821 brought a bountiful cargo from Hawaii to California. Grimes was cautious, particularly of the frigate *Reyna de los Angeles*, but spent two very successful months in ports between San Francisco and San Diego. In Santa Barbara he reported that goods sold to the commandant were duty free but private sales were charged twelve and a half percent.[17]

On February 24, 1821, Agustín de Iturbide, military leader of Mexican conservatives alienated by events in Spain, declared Mexico's independence, which Spain recognized in August of that year in the Treaty of Córdoba. For California this marked the end of the Spanish mercantilist isolation, but the new Mexican regime was not highly regarded by Californians, particularly after Iturbide, in May 1822, was crowned Agustín I, Emperor of Mexico. He was exiled ten months later and executed in 1824. When a new governor took office after California's first election, foreign trade was officially recognized as a part of life on the Pacific coast and imports were welcomed as a principal source of taxation.[18]

Import duties initially were moderate but were soon increased, and because they were enforced only at Monterey, Santa Barbara, San Pedro, and San Diego, smuggling flourished in places like San Juan Capistrano, Refugio, Santa Cruz, and San

Francisco. Thomas O. Larkin, later American consul and a pillar of Monterey society, confessed to evading port duties when they reached unreasonable levels, and Josiah Belden, for two years his agent in Santa Cruz, reported to Larkin, "The two Blls [barrels] liquor you sent I believe the Alcalde knows nothing about as yet, and I shall not let him know if I can help it. If he does I think I can mix it up so as to make it pass for country liquor."[19]

A similar evasion of liquor taxes in the spring of 1835 in Monterey was described by Richard Henry Dana in his book *Two Years Before the Mast.*

> ... [D]uring several successive nights a boat's crew were employed in smuggling ashore casks of spirit at a place a mile below the common landing. This was no breach of the laws on our part, for we had paid our duties and had liberty to sell and land our cargo wherever we chose; it was only done to accommodate purchasers who wished to avoid the excise which is laid upon every barrel of spirit opened for sale on shore. We pulled in for a small sand beach, and after taking a look around, landed and rolled the casks up on the sand, from whence they were always taken before morning. Two of the custom house officers themselves had their goods delivered in this manner ...."[20]

William Heath Davis, whom historian Bancroft described as "an honest, genial, industrious, and successful merchant," recalled that in May 1842 he was supercargo aboard Captain John Paty's *Don Quixote* inbound from Honolulu with a $20,000 cargo, on which he anticipated import duties equal to the value of the cargo. To avoid this excessive tax, Paty landed at Yerba Buena, which was not yet an official port of entry. Here Davis knew the sub-prefect, who came aboard for the ceremonial reminder that the official port of entry was Monterey. Davis, responding that a strong flood tide would not permit their immediate departure, promised to leave early the next day, and the sub-prefect assigned a guard overnight. The guard, also a friend, was fed, given cigars and brandy, and locked in a state-room while the crew worked through the night to row the silks, sugar, and other most valuable cargo to the waterfront ware-house of Davis's friend Nathan Spear.

By dawn half the cargo had been unloaded, in due course the guard was given twenty dollars in gold and set ashore, and the *Don Quixote* departed for Monterey, where Davis virtuously paid customs fees on what remained of his cargo. Several weeks later, armed with their customs receipts, the Americans returned to Spear's warehouse, where "transporting small lots at a time," they retrieved their silk and sugar and headed down the coast to their customers in the missions and ranchos of Santa Cruz, San Luis Obispo, and points south.[21]

William Heath Davis

Davis further recalled that "those who were transgressors of the law in this respect were not considered law-breakers in any odi-ous sense, but were in entire good standing in the community, and were, to a certain extent, benefiting the people and doing a service to the country" by keeping their prices down.[22]

Endnotes

1. Hubert Howe Bancroft, *The History of California*, 7 vols. (San Francisco: The History Company, 1890), 2:703.

2. Ibid., 2:35 ff.

3. C. M. Scammon, "Sea Otters," *Overland Monthly* 4 (1870): 25–30.

4. Magdalen Coughlin, "Boston Smugglers on the Coast (1797–1821): An Insight into the American Acquisition of California," *California Historical Society Quarterly* 46 (1967): 99–120.

5. Adele Ogden, *The California Sea Otter Trade, 1784–1848* (Berkeley: University of California Press, 1941), pp. 37–43.

6. Bancroft, 2:10–14.

7. H. W. S. Cleveland, *Voyages of a Merchant Navigator* (New York: Harper Brothers, 1886), p. 94; and Ogden, pp. 38–39.

8. Bancroft, 2:13.

9. Ogden, p. 42.

10. Ibid., pp. 46–47.

11. Ibid., pp. 49–50.

12. Ibid., pp. 58–59.

13. Charles F. Lummis, "Mr. Eayrs of Boston," *Out West* 30 (1909): 159–166.

14. Ibid.; Coughlin; and Ogden, p. 68.

15. Irving Berdine Richman, *California Under Spain and Mexico, 1535–1847* (Boston: Houghton Mifflin Co., 1965), pp. 185–209.

16. Ogden, pp. 62–63.

17. Ogden, pp. 80–85.

18. Charles E. Chapman, *A History of California; the Spanish Period* (New York: Macmillan, 1930), pp. 452–456; and Bancroft, 2:450–468.

19. George P. Hammond, ed., *The Larkin Papers: Personal, Business, and Official Correspondence of Thomas Oliver Larkin*, 10 vols. (Berkeley: University of California Press, 1951–1964), 1:251.

20. Richard Henry Dana, *Two Years Before the Mast*, ed. John Haskell Kemble (Los Angeles: Ward Ritchie Press, 1964), 1: 83.

21. William Heath Davis, *Seventy-five Years in California*. (San Francisco: John Howell, 1929), pp. 105–110.

22. Ibid., pp. 105–106.

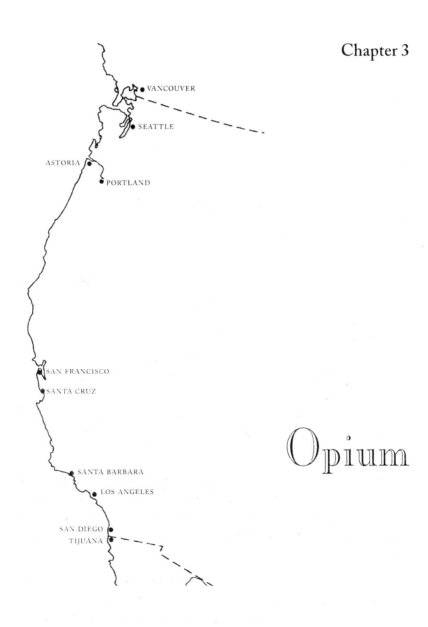

Chapter 3

VANCOUVER

SEATTLE

ASTORIA

PORTLAND

SAN FRANCISCO

SANTA CRUZ

Opium

SANTA BARBARA

LOS ANGELES

SAN DIEGO

TIJUANA

Every morning brought fresh complaints to the South Harbor Police Station of thefts along San Francisco's waterfront, the Embarcadero, particularly from owners of small boats moored at Mission Bay. In response, the police chief had established a new night patrol.

Rowing a big whitehall boat along the dark waterfront in search of looters was hard work and called for caution, stamina, and a sharp lookout. This was never more true than early on Wednesday morning, January 4, 1882, shortly after midnight. It was cold, raining, and the wind was blowing. Harbor Police Officers Jim Smith and Ned Egan cursed the rough bay waters and the downpour which soaked and chilled them. The north wind roared across the bay, and they could see very little through the rain.

They had been out a little over an hour and were rowing south toward the Pacific Mail Steamship Company dock at the end of First Street, wishing they were ashore indoors, when they saw what looked like another rowboat, not far from where the *City of Tokio* had been moored on the east side of the Pacific Mail Steamship Company pier since its arrival on Christmas day. On the other side of the pier lay the *City of Sydney*. At first they thought the rowboat might be a customs patrol assigned to watch for unloading of contraband through portholes.

Pulling closer, they could see that it was a whitehall rowboat, riding low in the water, with two men aboard. The men were rowing vigorously and seemed not to want company, which aroused the policemen's curiosity. Smith and Egan had little difficulty in catching up with the heavily loaded boat and called to the boatmen to stop.

Smith saw one of them throw something overboard and noticed that they had muffled oars. These observations, together with the fact that they were out on the bay on a night like this, made the policemen more than a little interested in knowing what their cargo was. Drawing their pistols, they boarded the other whitehall. The cargo consisted mostly of square packages wrapped in matting, which Smith thought from their size and weight might contain opium.

A Whitehall Boat

Egan handcuffed the rowers and attached a line to their boat. Smith rowed toward the Folsom Street wharf while Egan guarded the prisoners. It was not far but a hard pull through rough water, towing the heavy cargo. One of the prisoners offered to give the cargo to Egan if he would release them. Egan made it clear that he was not interested.

After making the boats fast at the foot of the Folsom Street steps, Smith marched the prisoners to the police station while Egan guarded the boats. The men identified themselves as James K. Kennedy, a ship's carpenter recently employed by the Pacific Mail Steamship Company, and William McDermott, known as Bricktop or Brick the Boatman, owner of the captured whitehall.

With their prisoners locked up, Smith and Egan returned to the Folsom steps with two other officers who helped them unload and examine the contraband. This was a matter of personal, as well as official, interest to Smith and Egan since they might receive as much as a third of its value as a reward for their vigilance.

Their examination of McDermott's boat produced two large rolls of silk and ninety-seven square packages wrapped in matting and tied with bamboo strips. Each package contained two tin containers, each weighing ten pounds and containing twenty small brass boxes of opium with Chinese labels. The total value of this ton of *kung yun* (Chinese smoking-opium) was later estimated at from $20,000 to $34,000.

As the opium was being unloaded a man approached the policemen, said his name was Kennedy, and offered first $2,000 then $10,000 to Egan to let the prisoners go. He was subsequently identified as Henry Kennedy, James Kennedy's brother, employed as steerage steward of the *Tokio*.[1]

Imported opium was not illegal in California in 1882 but was subject to a fifty percent federal import duty. This and a strong, steady demand were palpable incentives for smugglers. San Francisco had a number of opium dens, most of them in Chinatown. H. H. Kane, in his 1881 classic, *Opium Smoking in America and China*, estimated that twenty percent of the California Chinese smoked opium and that the number of Caucasian addicts was increasing rapidly.[2]

The use of opium in China, first brought from the Middle East, may have begun as early as the eighth century. The smoking of opium apparently began soon after the introduction of tobacco in the seventeenth century and developed fairly rapidly. Addiction was so widespread by 1729 that the emperor forbade its sale. By the end of the eighteenth century its cultivation and import were prohibited, but by that time aggressive British and Portuguese traders were so well established along China's southern coast that its importation continued. Further, it was the principal crop of the Ganges Valley in India and thus a major source of income for the British East India Company.

Chinese government confiscation of a British warehouse full of opium in Canton provide the *casus belli* for the First Opium War, which lasted from 1839 to 1842, intensified by various British assertions of extraterritoriality. It ended with Britain's capture of several cities in southern China and imposition of the Treaty of Nanking, at the end of August 1842, and the Treaty of the Bogue, 1843, which assessed a huge indemnity against the Ch'ing emperor and included cession to Britain of the territory of Hong Kong.

Over the next decade efforts by China, weakened by ineffective military forces, to resist foreign incursions had the perverse effect of stimulating British expansionism, which in 1856 precipitated the Second Opium War. France, citing the murder of a French missionary, shortly joined Britain in this effort to extend the economic outposts of empire. In 1858 China signed the Treaty of Tientsin, opening Peking to Western consulates and granting other major concessions. These measures were not popular, and the Treaty was not ratified. The Western allies resumed their hostilities, capturing Peking, and in 1860 China signed the Peking Convention, affirming the Tientsin Treaty and ending its efforts to prevent or limit the opium trade in China.[3]

Opium Smoking

Although opium addiction was early recognized as a serious problem by the Ch'ing dynasty, it was not until after the turn of the century that the drug was again prohibited in China. It is not surprising that Chinese immigrants to California toward the end of the nineteenth century found escape in their opium pipes from the harsh climate which produced the Chinese Exclusion Acts and the pervasive racial hostility which they faced on every hand.

One San Francisco store which supplied the opium dens was Kwong On and Company, at 796 Commercial Street. James Kennedy and a man who posted bond for him, Joseph Goetz, were known to be frequent visitors to Kwong On. Following the opium seizure on January 4, the Customs Service, the Port Office, and the United States Attorney were suddenly much interested in Kennedy, Goetz, and the Kwong On Company, as were the San Francisco newspapers. *The Daily Alta California* called it one of the most important seizures of contraband in the history of San Francisco Bay. *The New York Times* picked up the story a week later and, quoting the *San Francisco Examiner*, said it was the most important.[4]

The United States Marshal's office took custody of the opium, which was stored in the customs collector's warehouse. Because it was such a spectacular haul, everybody involved was much interested in knowing where it had originated. The most likely immediate source was the Pacific Mail Steamship Company's *City of Tokio*, recently arrived from Hong Kong.

Eleven customs inspectors assigned to supervise the unloading of the *Tokio* were under immediate suspicion, having apparently let a ton of contraband slip through their fingers, even though the stormy weather was an extenuating circumstance. Although Kennedy and McDermott were uninformative, the customs inspectors suggested that the drugs might have arrived on other ships and been stored in old hulks lying along the Embarcadero between Third and Fourth Streets.

The Steamer *City of Tokio*

Kennedy and McDermott, charged with smuggling and assisting in the concealment of contraband, spent the night in jail. However, Joseph Goetz and other friends and business associates appeared promptly the next day to post bail. Before the end of the week, Kennedy was asserting that the drugs were locally produced and that they were preparing to ship them to Hawaii aboard the steamer *City of Sydney*.

The opium containers were identical to some for which duty had been paid before they were unloaded from the *Tokio*, so the assertion that they were locally produced and the suggestion that they had been stored on abandoned ships were less than convincing. E. B. Matthews, captain of the night shift of customs inspectors aboard the *Tokio*, and several members of his staff were questioned at length but shed no new light on how the drugs were unloaded. Matthews was subsequently fired, although he protested that he was not on duty on the night in question.[5]

On Thursday, March 9, Assistant United States Attorney A. P. Van Duzer presented *The United States v. 3,880 Boxes of Opium* before Judge Ogden Hoffman in the U.S. District Court in San Francisco. He asserted that Kennedy and McDermott were members of a major smuggling ring which for several years had been bringing opium from Hong Kong to Kwong On and Company without paying import duty. In this most recent case alone their smuggling defrauded the government of $10,000.

Van Duzer reported that he and a deputy marshal, by waiting several hours at the stamp window at the post office, had intercepted a package of letters which he presented to the court, explaining that they revealed important new and definitive evidence in the case.

The package, brought to the post office by a Kwong On employee, was addressed to Tong San Wo, No. 1 Bonham Strand, Hong Kong. Among these letters Van Duzer found a note signed by James Kennedy, addressed to a man named Charlie, which established Kennedy's role as a principal in the organization. This communication also clearly implicated George Goetz, who signed a long letter dated March 18 addressed to "Friend Charley," describing the confiscation of the *City of Tokio* shipment and saying that he hoped they would soon succeed in retrieving it. It also included a letter signed by Lee Ah Wye, the head of Kwong On, which also acknowledged loss of the *Tokio* shipment, and revealed that Lee was somewhat less optimistic than Goetz about the outcome of the trial.

Kennedy, Goetz, and Lee had engaged two attorneys to defend them: George Washington Towle, later a San Francisco judge, and W. H. L. Barnes, known as General Barnes reflecting Civil War service as an officer in the Union Army. On the first day of the trial they produced two witnesses for the defense. The first was B. K. Sheridan, a drayman, who testified that on the night of January 3 he had hauled two loads of opium from the Tai Hung store, at 1014 Dupont Street, to James Kennedy at the wharf at the corner of Main and Bryant streets, from which Kennedy and McDermott were to transport it in McDermott's boat to the *City of Sydney*. The second defense witness, who identified himself as the ship's water tender, asserted that he had contracted to get the opium aboard, had opened the coal port a little before midnight on January 3 to receive it, and had subsequently seen the two rowboats pass the *Sydney*'s stern.

The covert movement of the opium was explained by the fact that because importation of the drug was prohibited in the Kingdom of Hawaii, the black-market price there was twice what they could get in San Francisco. This prohibition was confirmed by the Hawaiian consul, thus establishing the entrepreneurs' motivation for shipping the opium to Honolulu.[6]

Van Duzer asked for time to secure rebuttal witnesses. By the following week he was able to call an employee of Sheridan who testified that on the night of January 3 he slept in Sheridan's barn on Taylor Street, that he had the only key to the barn door, and that no horses had left the barn that night. Another witness reinforced the prosecution case by reporting that he was drinking with Sheridan in a Kearny Street saloon until 10:30 that night. An additional prosecution witness testified that he was night watchman on the pier at Main and Bryant, that he was on duty from early Tuesday night until 10:00 the next morning, that he always stopped horse-drawn vehicles entering the pier at night, and that none had entered on the night in question. Finally Van Duzer called another witness who corroborated the testimony about Sheridan and the Kearny Street bar.[7]

Testimony also established that James Kennedy had two brothers, Joseph, who was not directly implicated in the January incident, and Henry, who was steerage steward aboard the *Tokio* and who had appeared at the Folsom Street steps, according to Egan and Smith, while they were preparing to unload the opium, and had offered them the contraband and $10,000 if they would release the captives.[8]

Early on March 24, a dramatic interception was planned. Van Duzer, accompanied by the U.S. Attorney, Commissioner J. F. O'Beirne of the U.S. District Court, and various members of the U.S. Marshall's office and the U.S. Treasury, set out on the revenue cutter *Thomas Corwin* prepared to intercept the *Tokio*, due the next day in San Francisco. They planned to arrest Henry Kennedy and the *Tokio* purser, John M. Hennessey, both implicated in the January opium shipment by the Kwong On letters intercepted by Van Duzer. However, a brisk wind blowing in off the Pacific created a rough voyage, which thwarted the plans for the seasick dignitaries.

The next morning, after some difficulty with rough seas in boarding the *Tokio*, deputy marshals served arrest warrants on Kennedy and Hennessey.[9] Then shortly after the *Tokio* arrived at the Pacific Mail Steamship Company pier, Van Duzer and the officials were waiting, along with George Towle, the Kennedys' attorney, who took Henry Kennedy aside to bring him up to date on the course of the trial. Both Kennedy and Hennessey were escorted to the county jail where Joseph Kennedy, the third brother, presently arrived and posted $5,000 bail for his brother and the same amount for Hennessey.[10]

Assiduous customs agents searching the *Tokio* found two new caches of opium, one of four cases in an out-of-the-way pump shaft sleeve in the engine room and the other, of three cases, under a steel step plate. All of these cases, which bore the labels of Loon Took and Co. in Hong Kong, were identical to those seized from Kennedy and McDermott on January 4. This cleared up a previously vague point. One of Towle's defenses of the claim that the opium was produced in California was the presence in each tin container of a dated slip of San Francisco newspaper ostensibly too recent to have come from Hong Kong. Although the claimants had a generally weak case, this was one of their more effective points, which the prosecution was unable to answer satisfactorily, until now.[11]

Judge Ogden Hoffman delivered his decision on June 2, 1882, finding, in the government's favor, that the opium had been smuggled into San Francisco and condemned it to confiscation.[12]

The defense attorneys promptly initiated an appeal of Hoffman's decision, although it took them a year to present their case to the Ninth Circuit Court of Appeals. Judge Lorenzo Sawyer heard the case in March, 1883, and issued his decision on September 20 of that year. In a thirty-page decision Judge Sawyer acknowledged that attorneys Towle and Barnes constructed a full and careful case, noting that the District Court testimony filled 1700 pages, and the appeal an additional 800 pages. In deference to the imaginative and thorough defense, he said, in his decision:

> If I were required to determine the title of the property between two citizens, upon precisely the same case, I should say, but with considerable hesitation, that the preponderance of evidence is in favor of guilt in the transaction. Adopting the same rule as to the quantity of evidence requisite, while the point is not, in my mind, free from serious doubt, I find that the opium in question was smuggled into the port of San Francisco on the steam-ship *City of Tokio*, and that it was so smuggled with the actual intent to defraud the United States . . . . I find that there must be a decree for the government, condemning the opium as forfeited; and it is so ordered.[13]

There is no record of how much the Kennedys invested in the legal services of Towle and Barnes, to say nothing of defense witnesses and bail bonds, but those 3,880 cases of opium were an expensive piece of bad luck. Whether this discouraged them from further smuggling or just caused them to be more careful, there is no public record of their heavy investment in imported opium after 1882.

In 1909 Congress passed a law prohibiting the importation of smoking opium and closely controlling import of opium "for medicinal purposes ... for the treatment or prevention of diseases of man or other animal."[14] This prohibition did not immediately diminish the demand for the drug in San Francisco's Chinatown, but it produced a dramatic increase in its market value. On January 19, 1911, customs inspectors made a major opium haul on the Pacific Mail Steamship Company liner *Korea*, finding 795 tins of smoking opium secreted in various locations aboard the ship. The following day they burned 750 pounds, which they valued at $60,000, an eight-fold increase in value since the *Tokio* incident.[15]

There had been a corresponding increase in the risks involved in smuggling. Captain J. W. Saunders of the *Korea* was threatened with a statutory maximum fine of $15,000, recommended to the secretary of the Treasury by the San Francisco customs office, and there was a general tightening of customs inspections, particularly at night.[16]

Some new developments regarding opium were now changing the drug scene. The refinement of opium had begun in 1806 when a German pharmacist named Friederich Wilhelm Serturner extracted morphine from it by dissolving it in liquid ammonia. During the nineteenth century various morphine products developed, culminating in 1898 in the extraction of heroin, roughly four times as powerful as morphine and extremely addictive. Its manufacture was banned in the United States in 1924.[17] By the 1960s heroin had become the predominant American street drug.

Raw opium had all but disappeared from the market in California when suddenly in December 1987, more than a century after the *City of Tokio* affair, postal inspectors began to find opium in quantities large enough to worry federal officials. It arrived in packages mailed by people in Thailand and addressed to their relatives, Hmong and Mien immigrants, many of them living in California's central valley. Although the quantities were small by comparison with those of cocaine, hashish, and heroin shipments, the packages contained five and ten-pound bricks of pure opium, and the aggregate for the year in postal packages alone was over a thousand pounds, more than a threefold increase in one year. With a street value which the U.S. Drug Enforcement Administration (DEA) estimated at $110,000 per pound, it was a profitable import.[18]

The DEA was puzzled by this resurgence of opium imports, according to a reporter for the *San Jose Mercury News* who quoted one agent as saying that recipients, like 42-year-old Chao Thong Saechao, a Mien immigrant living in Sacramento, arrested when she received a package of opium addressed to her, were "good, law-abiding, well-behaved people" not engaged in crimes of violence or drug sales. The reporter talked to one Hmong authority who said that most of the Hmong and Mien had been subsistence farmers and that for "almost any kind of flu, illness, or pain the elders tended to utilize opium [from poppies they had grown themselves] as one of their principal medicines."[19]

Although small shipments of raw opium continue to arrive in the California mail, its weight and limited potency make it a much less concealable — or profitable — import than heroin, that opium derivative that has become a new focus for smugglers.

Endnotes

1. *United States v. 3,880 Boxes of Opium*, 23 F. 369 (9th Cir. 1883).

2. Harry H. Kane, *Opium Smoking in America and China* (New York: G. P. Putnam's Sons, 1882).

3. Ibid., 15; and "The Opium Trade," *Living Age* 35 (1852): 546–552.

4. *San Francisco Chronicle* 5 January 1882, p. 4; *The Daily Alta California* 5 January 1882, p. 1; *San Francisco Call* 5 January 1882, p. 3; and *The New York Times* 14 January 1882, p. 3.

5. *San Francisco Examiner* 29 March 1882, p. 3.

6. Ibid., 11 March 1882, p. 1; and *3,880 Boxes of Opium v. United States*, p. 372.

7. *The Daily Alta California* 18 March 1882, p. 1.

8. *3,880 Boxes of Opium v. United States*, 369.

9. *San Francisco Call* 27 March 1882, p. 2.

10. *San Francisco Examiner* 27 March 1882, p. 3.

11. Ibid., 29 March 1882, p. 3.

12. *San Francisco Call* 3 June 1882, p. 3.

13. *United States v. 3,880 Boxes of Opium*, 396–397.

14. *San Francisco Chronicle* 28 March 1909, p. 39.

15. Ibid., 20 January 1911, p. 15.

16. Ibid., 24 June 1911, p. 16.

17. George R. Gay and E. Leong Way, "Pharmacology of the Opiate Narcotics," *It's So Good, Don't Even Try It Once: Heroin in Perspective*, ed. David E. Smith and George R. Gay (New York: Prentice-Hall, 1972), p. 45 ff.

18. *San Jose Mercury News* 24 December 1987, sec. A, p. 1.

19. Ibid.

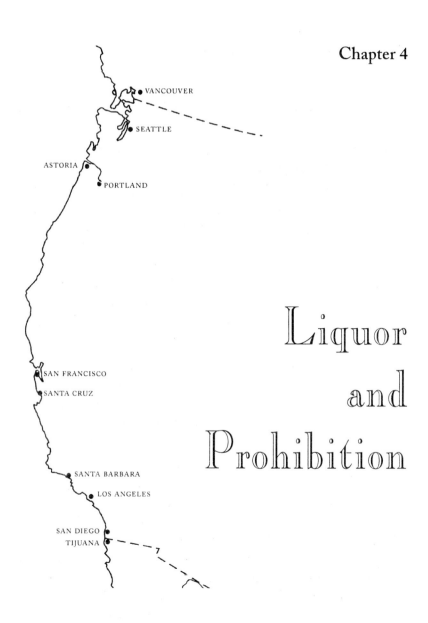

Chapter 4

Liquor

and

Prohibition

I t was midnight, and at a signal flashed from shore the motor launch *Kagome*, showing no lights, purred slowly in from the mouth of the Noyo River to the fish dock. It was a clear, cold December night, 1932, and by starlight the land crew hauled 200 cases of Canadian whisky to waiting trucks and brought fresh meat and vegetables to the boat, which promptly put to sea.

A fortnight earlier the Canadian motor launch, fast enough to outrun the Coast Guard, had brought several loads of liquor from a ship anchored off Point Reyes to Salt Point, farther south, near the old Russian outpost of Fort Ross. The *Kagome* had barely escaped as federal officers closed in, arresting four men and capturing two trucks, four cars, and 500 cases of Scotch. Approaching the Christmas season the smugglers had an abundance of holiday orders, but though the *Kagome* had an experienced California pilot to find new landing places, the Coast Guard, Prohibition Bureau, and local law enforcement agencies were finding them, too, and making life very difficult.[1]

By the early 1900s, the Anti-Saloon League, the Women's Christian Temperance Union, and the Prohibition Party had been fighting drunkenness for many years, but it may well have been the urbane elders of the American Medical Association (AMA) who finally tipped the Congressional scales toward Prohibition.

At its annual meeting in 1917 the AMA House of Delegates "... Resolved, That the American Medical Association opposes the use of alcohol as a beverage ...."[2] By the end of that year, Congress enacted the Eighteenth Amendment to the Constitution, prohibiting the "manufacture, sale, or transportation of intoxicating liquors within, the importation thereof into, or the exportation thereof from the United States and all territory subject to the jurisdiction thereof for beverage purposes ...."[3]

There had been precedent-setting state laws as far back as the first half of the nineteenth century. In April 1838 Massachusetts passed a law prohibiting the sale of distilled spirits in containers of less than fifteen gallons (repealed two years later), and Maine passed a prohibition law in 1846 which established a pattern followed by thirteen other states which enacted similar laws within the next decade.[4]

SINGIN' IN THE RAIN
—Evans in the Columbus *Dispatch*.

Prohibition Cartoon

By the end of the First World War, Prohibition was a major issue in American politics. Republicans were generally supportive of Prohibition; many Democrats opposed it. Protestants were predominantly dry; Catholics tended to be more tolerant. Both sides were predictably influenced by temperance and liquor lobbies. The Eighteenth Amendment, passed by Congress in December 1917, was ratified by the states in less than two years. Its enforcement was elaborated by a law introduced by Congressman Andrew J. Volstead of Minnesota. Congress overrode President Wilson's veto in October 1919, and the Volstead Act, also called the Prohibition Enforcement Act, took effect on January 16, 1920.[5]

Humbert S. Nelli, professor of history at the University of Kentucky and an authority on American crime syndicates, says:

> When the Eighteenth Amendment and the Prohibition Enforcement Act (or Volstead Act) went into effect on January 16, 1920, the American public and its elected officials had no conception of the violence, corruption, and disrespect for the law that the so-called noble experiment would cause or encourage. In fact national prohibition was ushered in with a great deal of optimism and hope . . . .[6]

If the new laws had any effect upon the public thirst, they appeared to increase rather than to diminish it. Nelli further recalls: "Within days, police departments were carrying out raids in an effort to end the growing and highly profitable traffic in illicit alcohol. Dry laws or not, Americans wanted their drinks and were ready to do business with anyone who could supply them."[7]

Because established American breweries, wineries, and distilleries were closed, the public taste for alcohol fostered a thirteen-year orgy of moonshine, near beer, bathtub gin, and other toxic fluids. Bootleggers with access to industrial alcohol were freed of the cost and complications of importing bottled booze. However, their quality control left something to be desired. "The alcohol often needed processing (caramel, creosote, and prune juice could be added, for instance, to give the taste and color of scotch)."[8]

The Bronfman family of Canada, founders of the Seagram's empire of distilleries, warehouses, and billion-dollar entertainment companies, played an important role in the humanitarian effort to save American topers from bathtub gin, home brew, and synthetic scotch. The Bronfmans, veterans of a successful mail-order business when Canada's prairie provinces went dry, were soon supplying potable rum, scotch, and Canadian whiskey to bootleggers in Minnesota, North Dakota, and Montana. With headquarters in Nova Scotia and British Columbia, they were able to ship Good Stuff, as professionally made liquor was called, to California and New York.[9]

Because the roads across the U.S. and Canadian border were fairly easily controlled and because the Good Stuff was bulky, heavy, and in fragile containers, ships and boats soon became the principal mode of transport, first on the Great Lakes and then along both the Atlantic and Pacific coasts.

The drinkers of San Francisco and Los Angeles were the two principal markets in the west, and the combination of thirst, greed, ingenuity, and easy money kept the Good Stuff flowing into San Diego, San Pedro, San Francisco, and onto dark, quiet beaches up and down the Pacific coast. Monterey Bay was one of the preferred areas for landing Canadian liquor. It had broad, gentle beaches, adequate roads, and fewer inquisitive people than San Francisco Bay and the Peninsula. Moss Landing, Capitola, and Davenport Landing all saw their share of night landings.

A major supplier of liquor was the Consolidated Exporters Corporation, Limited, of Vancouver, British Columbia, Canada. Two of its principals, George W. Norgan (whose obituary in 1964 said he was one of Canada's wealthiest men) and Albert L. McLennan, were indicted (though never convicted) in November 1926 by a federal grand jury in San Francisco along with several of their shippers, a score of their agents, and a scattering of customers in the San Francisco Bay area.[10]

One of Consolidated Exporters' ships, the schooner *Malahat*, made several trips from Vancouver in 1924, nominally bound for Colombia but frequently found stationed near the Farallon Islands twenty-seven miles west of San Francisco. There, in February 1924, as reported in the 1926 indictment, it delivered 500 cases of liquor to Henry W. Lyon. Under cover of darkness Lyon transported it in his motor launch *B-176* to Tomales Bay, for transshipment to the city. Other Consolidated Exporters' ships operating off the coast of California were the *Coal Harbor* and the *Federalship*, eventually apprehended by the Coast Guard, and the *Norburn*, which was not.[11]

The Canadian Freighter *Federalship*, **May 1927**

Another *Malahat* customer was Sam Terry who in September 1924 acquired a fast motor launch called the *Viz 4*, which he renamed the *Acajutla*. He hired Edward W. Magruder as master and sent him to meet the *Malahat* out beyond the Farallons. Magruder picked up 450 cases of whisky, wine, brandy, gin, and champagne, which he delivered to Russian Gulch, convenient to the highway north of Jenner, on the Mendocino County coast.[12]

The *Malahat* had competition during much of 1924 from the British steamer *Ardenza*, from Leith, Scotland, which came through the Panama Canal to set up shop off Half Moon Bay, where in due course it disposed of its cargo of 25,000 cases of Scotch whisky, much of it to motor launches from San Francisco Bay. Coast Guard Commander Malcolm Willoughby, in his reminiscence, *Rum War at Sea*, recalled, "It is incredible to suppose that her presence and business were not known. It was said that contact boats passed through the Golden Gate at certain hours when a particular official on duty found it profitable to be unobserving!" Having sold its cargo, the *Ardenza* left California waters for Vancouver, where it was less welcome, was seized, sold, and sent back to Scotland.[13]

Rumrunning was a quiet business, landings were at night, and the only lasting records of these transactions resulted when one or more of the importers were apprehended. Perhaps the most famous capture was of the unfortunate *Quadra*.

Although Consolidated Exporters' big ships generally stayed well out in international waters, the 683-ton steamer *Quadra*, with a half-million-dollar cargo of 12,000 cases of whisky and champagne, had ventured close to the Farallons where, on October 12, 1924, it delivered fifty sacks of liquor to the fishing boat *C-55*.

The Coast Guard cutter *Shawnee*, commanded by Lieutenant Commander Charles Howell, had been looking for the *Quadra*. The previous night the Coast Guard had apprehended the motorboat *903-B*, entering the Golden Gate channel with a full cargo of gin, brandy, whisky, and vermouth.

Captain Howell shortly succeeded in capturing both vessels, taking the small craft first, then easily overtaking the steamer, by then westward bound at full speed. Captain George Ford of the *Quadra* refused Howell's order to take it in to San Francisco under its own power and likewise refused inspection of his manifest. Howell arrested him and his crew, and the cutter towed both vessels in through the Golden Gate. The *Quadra* was moored near Hunters Point after its cargo was removed to the appraiser's warehouse.[14]

The trial in the U.S. District Court four months later revealed an elaborate organization extending from Vancouver south to Los Angeles. Ford and two principal Consolidated Exporters' agents in San Francisco, Vincent Quartararo and Charles Belanger, received two-year prison sentences and substantial fines. The first and second mates of the *Quadra* were given shorter sentences, the chief engineer a $500 fine, and the rest of the crew released.[15]

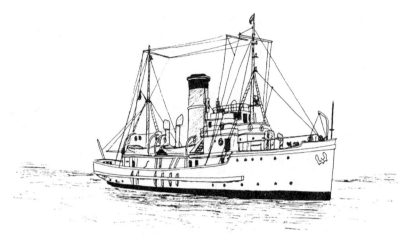

The U.S. Coast Guard Cutter *Shawnee*, **(ca 1925)**

The convictions of Ford, Quartararo, and Belanger were appealed to the Ninth Circuit Court, then to the United States Supreme Court — primarily on the question of whether the capture had been within U.S. territorial waters — but were sustained at both levels.[16]

One minor defense claim accepted by the Ninth Circuit revealed an ingenious device for identifying the skippers of the landing craft and the liquor which they were to deliver. Quartararo wrote his liquor invoices on dollar bills, which were cut in two, half delivered in advance to the ship's captain, the other half presented by the speedboat captain on the pickup rendezvous. Eighty-three of these bills, demonstrably inscribed by Vincent Quartararo and pasted together after the deliveries, were offered by the thrifty bootleggers to the Bank of Italy as legal tender and promptly fell into government hands. The Ninth Circuit

Court disallowed them as evidence because they were not turned in until a month after the rumrunning ring was broken.[17]

To avoid this kind of expense and discomfort, rumrunners frequently had to invest generously in gifts of money and whisky for officials responsible for various aspects of enforcing the Volstead Act. Bribery was one of the established expenses of the business. Its cost was somewhat unpredictable, depending on the risks involved, but bootlegging, like the Californians' evasion of early nineteenth century Spanish trade restrictions, was not in itself regarded as a seriously reprehensible crime. Its corrosive influence on law enforcement was frequently tolerated until it became blatant or violent.

The late Malio Stagnaro, for many years doyen of the Santa Cruz fishing fleet, recalled rumrunning and bribery during the 1920s when the central coast played an important part in what had become a large and lucrative maritime industry.

> Say they were paying $40 a case, and they'd bring in 500 cases; they'd make $20 a case, and they had a profit of $10,000 a night. And some of those boats were in and out every night. So you see it would be nothing for them to clean up $300,000 a month.

Stagnaro remembered seeing liquor unloaded occasionally on the Santa Cruz municipal pier, and although asserting that the Stagnaro brothers stuck to fishing and excursion boats, he said he knew most of the San Francisco Bay area rumrunners, many of whom were either Sicilian or Neapolitan. Stagnaro had a good notion not only of what the rumrunners earned but also of what they had to pay for impunity. He recalled that $2 or $3 a case was a reasonable range for hush money. At $3, a load of 500 cases could cost $1,500, shared among farmers, pier owners, and law enforcement officers.[18]

In May 1932, William J. Walker, chief of police in Santa Cruz, and John C. Geyer, commissioner of Public Health and Safety, were caught accepting bribes made in marked bills of modest denomination by two private detectives thought to be agents of a local reform group called the Good Government League. The Good Government League had been formed by Protestant clergymen alarmed by the pervasive influence of bootlegging and gambling in Santa Cruz County.

John C. Geyer

William J. Walker

Both Geyer and Walker confessed that for two years they had been dividing some $350 a month in bribes, which Walker admitted collecting and sharing fifty-fifty with Geyer. Walker was promptly sentenced to one to fourteen years in prison, but Geyer, on the advice of an aggressive attorney, repudiated his confession, miraculously stayed out of jail, and kept his seat on the city council, although not as commissioner of Public Safety.[19]

The Prohibition Bureau, the troubled federal bureaucracy with principal responsibility for enforcing the Volstead Act, was for most of its existence a part of the Treasury Department and was generally outnumbered, outgunned, and outspent in its contest with the rumrunners. Maritime smuggling brought the Coast Guard into the business of prohibition enforcement, a new role with unwelcome effects on an organization whose primary concern had heretofore been maritime safety. The immensity of the enforcement task far exceeded the capacity of both the Bureau and the Coast Guard. Because they had to counter the violent tactics of organized crime, they were criticized both for being too tough and for being ineffectual. After machine-gun fire from the Coast Guard cutter *CG290* killed three men aboard the rumrunner *Black Duck* on December 29, 1929, in Narragansett Bay, New York Congressman Fiorello LaGuardia complained:

> The Coast Guard ten years ago was one of the finest branches of the government service. The honesty, the courage, the cleanliness of Coast Guard men was traditional and held up as an example to every other branch of government.
>
> As soon as that service came in contact with Prohibition, it became contaminated. Look at it now; what Prohibition has done to the Coast Guard it will do to the Department of Justice within a short time after that department is cursed with the duty of Prohibition enforcement.[20]

LaGuardia, who was a passionate opponent of Prohibition, wrongly charged that the Coast Guard misappropriated the bootleg booze aboard the *Black Duck*. Still, the *Black Duck* incident stirred public anger against the Coast Guard comparable to that against the FBI and the U.S. Bureau of Alcohol, Tobacco, and Firearms in 1994 following the Branch Davidian episode.

In the early years of Prohibition small bootleggers flourished, but by 1923 organizations like the Torrio gang in Chicago and the Sicilian Mafia were eliminating competition by the simple and direct means of machine-gunning their competitors. During the late 1920s in Chicago hundreds of gangsters died in this guerrilla warfare. On the high seas the casualties were fewer, but rumrunners were on their own. Bold and resourceful hijackers were richly rewarded and generally avoided prosecution.

Captain Bill McCoy, perhaps most famous of East Coast rumrunners, whose pride in the quality of his cargo gave rise to the phrase "the real McCoy," always had an adequate arsenal aboard and was habitually alert to the threat of hijackers. He later recalled that "while selling liquor on the Row, all of us went armed, and submachine guns were hidden in the furled sails."[21]

In the book *The Black Ships: Rumrunners of Prohibition*, author Everett Allen recounts the hijacking of the *Mulhouse*.

> A vessel of about 1,000 tons, of French registry and like many another in the same traffic, shabby and ill kept .... [She] anchored off the Jersey Coast to sell a cargo of liquor — thousands of cases — reportedly worth about a half-million dollars. She had been there a week when she was boarded by a boatload of pirates, thirty of them, armed with guns and knives. Under threats of shooting to kill, they rounded up the *Mulhouse*'s crew, and locked them in the forecastle, under guard.

They then proceeded to remove the cargo to their several schooners, sold part of it to visiting customers, and drank some of it themselves. The *Mulhouse* crew was finally released, their holds empty, to return to France, poorer but wiser.[22]

The Eighteenth Amendment was a major issue in the party conventions of 1932, and its repeal was one of the principal planks of the Democratic platform, which contributed to Franklin Roosevelt's election as president. Both houses of Congress promptly passed the Twenty-first Amendment, motivated not only by the unfortunate biproducts of Prohibition but also by the hope that repeal would create new jobs in the depth of the Depression.[23]

Even the end of Prohibition did not stem the momentum of West Coast rumrunning. Although repeal removed the sanctions against the importation of liquor, there were import duties and taxes to be paid. In the waning days of the Depression evasion of these assessments was enough to promise smugglers a modest livelihood, albeit less than during Prohibition. In the early hours of October 28, 1933, for example, federal agents from San Francisco intercepted a liquor landing near Stewart's Point, on the Mendocino County coast north of Fort Ross. The smugglers shot and seriously wounded Agent Norman D. Austin. A fellow agent received a grazing head wound and was taken hostage, then released near Bodega Bay. The smugglers lost most of their liquor but escaped with one carload.[24]

Three years later Sherwood Johnston, a wealthy Hillsborough businessman, John C. Marino, a San Francisco liquor dealer, his agent Alfred Hubbard, and several others were indicted for smuggling to California 1,000,000 gallons of alcohol over a two-year period, aboard Marino's ship *Yukatrivol* and W. W. Keene's *Molokai*, from Los Mochis, Mexico, where Johnston's United Sugar Company had a refinery and distillery. One witness testified that it "was a very simple procedure to get alcohol out of Los Mochis by billing it as rice and corn." Marino and Hubbard received two-year sentences. Johnston and nine other defendants, then living in Mexico, remained expatriates.[25]

In the early years of Prohibition bootlegging had been much easier and safer than it was during the Depression. In the years just before repeal, rumrunning in California was neither easy nor safe. Law enforcement was benefiting not only from a decade of hard experience but also from increasingly active help from the public. Public tolerance was wearing thin, not so much to contraband liquor itself as to its side effects — murder, hijacking, conspiracy, and public corruption.

The shore of Monterey Bay was thinly populated, and its beaches had for some years been favorites for night landing. Leslie Thornewill owned a Santa Cruz trucking company suspected of transporting Canadian liquor from Monterey Bay beaches to San Francisco. When he left his wealthy, middle-aged common-law wife, Cora Mead, for a younger woman, it was reported that she threatened to expose his rumrunning. On September 26, 1928, shortly after a frightened phone call, she was found in her kitchen with the top of her head blown off, a .30 caliber rifle lying nearby. The sheriff declared that it was suicide, but a suspicious coroner's jury decided it was murder, by "party or parties unknown." Thornewill was jailed briefly but released to die a year later, shot by a jealous new wife.[26] No one was convicted of either Mead's or Thornewill's death, but they were of the Prohibition era and typical victims of its many violent and mysterious crimes.

Prohibition lasted until December 5, 1933, when Utah ratified the Twenty-first Amendment, repealing the Eighteenth.

Endnotes

1. Frank J. Hyman, *Historic Writings: a Recording of Facts and Description Concerning the Area on the Mendocino Coast in and around Fort Bragg, California* (n.p., 1966), pp. 22–29.

2. "Report of Reference Committee on Legislation," *Journal of the American Medical Association* 68 (1917): 1837; and "Putting Science in the Constitution: the Prohibition Experience," *Law, Alcohol, and Order: Perspectives on National Prohibition*, Contributions in American History, ed. David E. Kyvig, no. 110 (Westport, CT: Greenwood Press, 1985), pp. 20–31.

3. Andrew Sinclair, *Prohibition: the Era of Excess* (Boston: Little, Brown & Co., 1962), p. 165.

4. John Allen Krout, *The Origins of Prohibition* (New York: Russell & Russell, 1966), pp. 262–268; and Sinclair, p. 4.

5. Sinclair, pp. 162–170; Humbert S. Nelli, "American Syndicate Crime: a Legacy of Prohibition," *Law, Alcohol, and Order: Perspectives on National Prohibition*, Contributions in American History, ed. David E. Kyvig, no. 110 (Westport, CT: Greenwood Press, 1985), 124–125; and Page Smith, *America Enters the World* (New York: McGraw-Hill, 1985), p. 787.

6. Nelli, pp. 124–125.

7. Ibid.

8. Mark H. Haller, "Bootleggers as Businessmen: From City Slums to City Builders," *Law, Alcohol, and Order: Perspectives on National Prohibition*, Contributions in American History, ed. David E. Kyvig, no. 110 (Westport, CT: Greenwood Press, 1985), p. 140

9. Ibid., pp. 142–145.

10. *United States v. Ferris*, 18523 F. 21 (Dist. Ct. 1926).

11. Ibid., p. 6.

12. Ibid.

13. Malcolm F. Willoughby, *Rum War at Sea* (Washington, D.C.: U.S. Coast Guard, 1964), p. 78.

14. Ibid., p. 81.

15. *San Francisco Chronicle* 4 April 1925, p. 2.

16. *Ford v. United States*, 47 Sup. Ct. 531 (1927); and *Ford v. United States*, 10 F. 2d 341 (1926).

17. Ibid., 10 F. 349.

18. Malio J. Stagnaro, "Malio J. Stagnaro, the Santa Cruz Genovese," interview by Elizabeth Spedding Calciano, manuscript, 1975, McHenry Library Special Collections, University of California, Santa Cruz, pp. 235–247.

19. *Santa Cruz Sentinel* 18 May 1932, p. 1 ff.; 19 May p. 1 ff.; 15 June 1932, p. 1 ff.; and *Santa Cruz Evening News* 19 May 1932, p. 1 ff.

20. Everett S. Allen, *The Black Ships; Rumrunners of Prohibition* (Boston: Little, Brown & Co., 1979), pp. 261–268.

21. Ibid., p. 25.

22. Ibid., pp. 25–27.

23. Sinclair, pp. 382–391.

24. *San Francisco Chronicle* 20 October 1933, p. 1.

25. *Los Angeles Times* 3 September 1936, p. 3; 4 September 1936, p. 2; 22 September 1936, p. 8; and *The New York Times* 9 August 1939, p. 17.

26. *San Francisco Chronicle* 2 January 1930, p. 1.

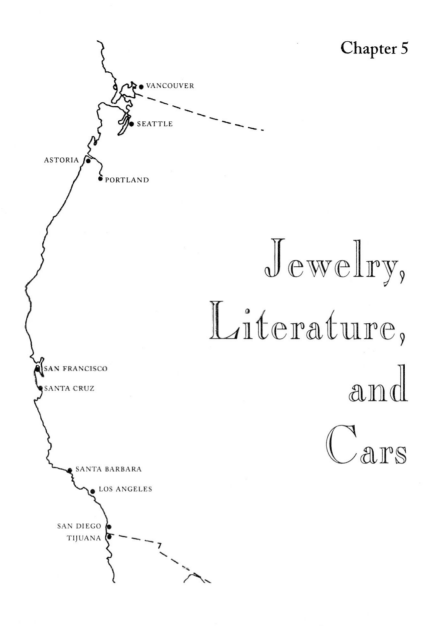

Chapter 5

Jewelry,

Literature,

and

Cars

In early December 1938 radio comedian George Burns received word in Hollywood that he was in trouble. He was under federal indictment in New York City for smuggling. Burns promptly flew to New York. There he appeared before Judge William Bondy of the U.S. District Court and pleaded guilty to charges of smuggling $4,885 worth of jewelry into the United States as gifts for his wife, Gracie Allen. At the trial, which lasted almost a month, Burns shared the uncomfortable spotlight with a professional smuggler named Albert N. Chapereau, who plied his trade under the protection of a Nicaraguan diplomatic passport as a commercial attaché of the Nicaraguan Consulate General in New York.

Chapereau, who was the actual importer of the Burns's contraband jewelry, as well as of high fashion women's clothes, had performed similar services for Jack Benny and for Elma N. Lauer, wife of New York Supreme Court Justice Edgar J. Lauer, among others. Burns and Benny were fined and put on probation, but Mrs. Lauer, who had been caught evading customs once before, received a three-month jail sentence, which caused her husband to resign in disgrace. *The New York Times* reported that Burns paid $17,770 in fines and import duties. His wife Gracie was permitted to keep her jewelry, two bracelets and a diamond ring, but Judge Bondy gave Burns a few bad moments when he sentenced him to a year in jail, paused for effect, then suspended the sentence. Jack Benny was tried later, also as a client of Chapereau, and fined a somewhat smaller amount. Chapereau went to prison for two years.[1]

Jewelry, because of its value and ease of concealment, has since time immemorial lent itself to smuggling. It is therefore one of the commodities, along with narcotics, for which customs agents are generally most vigilant.

Because veterans of World War II came home on troop ships by the thousands, they were less vigilantly examined by customs when they disembarked than were civilian tourists. The safe deposit boxes of many veterans of overseas service may still contain small but valuable souvenirs, of vague provenance, imported in duffel bags.

None of these souvenirs, however, is likely to compare, either in quality or quantity, with Colonel Murray's diamonds. Colonel Edward Jackson Murray of Palo Alto, an infantryman whose Silver Star, Bronze Star, and Legion of Merit attested to his distinguished service in the Philippines (first as commander of the 160th Infantry Regiment, then as military commander of the Island of Panay) was assigned in 1945 by the Supreme Commander for the Allied Powers as custodian of the Bank of Japan, a post in which he served for two years.

Colonel Murray, fifty-five years old, a veteran of World War I and a bridge engineer in the California Public Works Department until his call to active duty in the National Guard in 1941, elected to retire from the army in 1947, and he had just returned to California aboard a military transport, disembarking at the Oakland Army Base, on February 3, 1947, when he was detained by customs agents. As the result of information which the Army had relayed from Tokyo, they questioned him at some length, finally searched him, and removed four diamonds, which they valued at $10,000, from his watch pocket.[2]

During his interview with the Customs Service, Murray admitted that these were not his only Japanese souvenirs; in March 1946 he had brought more gems home to his wife, Lodema, and put them in a Wells Fargo safe deposit box. News of Colonel Murray's diamonds was cabled to the Supreme Commander, and MacArthur's headquarters ordered his arrest and confinement to his home in Palo Alto. The safe deposit box proved to contain 532 stones, most of them diamonds, the largest, weighing 10.5 karats, judged to be worth $6,000, and another set in a gold ring. There were also a dozen emeralds, a large ruby, and seventeen semi-precious stones. The initial appraisal was $210,000.

When this news reached Tokyo, MacArthur ordered Murray confined at Fort Mason, San Francisco's port of embarkation.

In deference to his rank and distinguished combat service, his confinement was in the hostess house rather than in the post stockade.

Here, awaiting air transportation back to Japan, he was interviewed by reporters to whom he described the diamonds as "souvenirs," but he declined to answer questions about where he got them. He did recall that "jewels and precious metals were found all over Japan ... hidden and tucked away in warehouses and other places" and suggested that in the early days of the occupation, American servicemen had found many valuables. "'Just like a big Easter-egg hunt?' a reporter asked. 'Well, yes,' Colonel Murray replied."[3]

The Army court-martial, over which Major General William Chase presided, opened on April 14, in Yokohama. The prosecutor charged Murray with misappropriating the jewels from the vaults of the Bank of Japan and smuggling them into California. Murray pleaded not guilty. The prosecution further revealed that he had sold four of the stones and produced a $13,000 check made to Mrs. Murray, drawn on the account of a San Francisco diamond broker. The defense counsel declined to put Murray on the stand, saying, "There is little he would add."[4]

Colonel Edward J. Murray

On May 29 the court found Colonel Murray guilty and sentenced him to dismissal from the Army and ten years at hard labor. Its only concession to the defense was to reduce the valuation of his diamonds from $210,000 to $92,000.[5] On July 15 Lieutenant General Robert L. Eichelberger, Eighth Army commander, who had awarded the Legion of Merit to Murray a year earlier, reduced his sentence to eight years.[6]

After sixteen months in the Eighth Army stockade in Tokyo, Murray was returned to Fort Mason aboard the *General Hodges* and confined at Camp Stoneman, north of San Francisco. The adjutant general reduced his sentence to five years.[7] His energetic attorney, James T. Davis, filed a petition for a writ of habeas corpus with the U.S. District Court in San Francisco on November 15, 1948, arguing that Murray was held incommunicado for a month before his trial and denied choice of his defense counsel. Davis's principal argument, however, was that General Chase, who was both president of the court-martial and Murray's immediate predecessor as custodian of the Bank of Japan's vaults, should have disqualified himself from the court because of "personal interest." Davis presented an affidavit from Murray's Yokohama defense counsel saying that Chase had "acted as both prosecutor and judge."[8]

At a hearing before Judge Michael J. Roche on March 28, 1949, Murray for the first time declared that the stones had been delivered to him in his Tokyo hotel room one autumn evening in 1945. They were in an envelope, he said, brought by a "slim Oriental." He assumed they were a gift in appreciation of his rescuing some people from robbers "on a dark road one evening." He thought perhaps the robbers were diamond hijackers. He testified further that he didn't realize, since they were gifts, that he owed duty on them. General Chase was summoned from Atlanta to testify, denied that he had been prejudiced, but admitted seeking additional evidence from the prosecution.[9]

Judge Roche denied the petition, and Davis appealed to the Ninth Circuit Court of Appeals. On January 20, 1950, the appellate court also denied the appeal, having ascertained that Colonel Murray had applied to the Army for, and in December 1949 had been granted, a parole. Although the parole ended his incarceration, Murray's original sentence had imposed a dishonorable discharge with forfeiture of all pay and allowances; these were not restored by the parole. Davis's final effort was to petition the U.S. Supreme Court for a writ of certiorari, an attempt to overturn the original court-martial decision. The Supreme Court denied the petition on June 5, 1950. Veterans' Administration records indicate that Colonel Murray died on May 1, 1953.[10]

Smuggling was not limited to jewelry, of course. During World War II the U.S. Customs Service, charged with confiscating treasonable or seditious material, became concerned with the amount of incoming erotic literature and photographs. After confiscating a returning European traveller's copy of Henry Miller's *Tropic of Cancer* in 1960, the Customs Service was challenged by the American Civil Liberties Union, beginning a series of court cases which undertook the complicated process of defining pornography and which greatly expanded the range of the acceptable. During this process, however, many copies of Miller's works, as well as books by James Joyce, D. H. Lawrence, and other authors whose writing ventured into the erotic, were tucked undeclared into the suitcases of returning travelers, and many escaped Customs scrutiny.[11]

It is interesting to note that a 1998 American poll chose James Joyce's *Ulysses*, first published in France in 1920, as the best of the hundred best novels of this century, recalling that when it first appeared it was branded as obscene and that copies of a literary magazine which published one chapter were burned by the U.S. Post Office.[12]

By comparison with other forms of criminal endeavor, smuggling has always shown unusual imagination and ingenuity. A recent example of this was the arrest in 1994 of a ring of southern California entrepreneurs operating from a bookstore in Torrance owned by Norman Kwon. Their specialty was the export to China of expensive stolen cars.

Mercedes, Lexus, BMW, and Jaguar were favorites in the Asian market, and a U.S. Customs inspector estimated that of the 300,000 cars worth $1.5 billion stolen in California in 1994, 60,000 were exported, to be sold abroad at substantial profit.[13]

Mark Bousian of the *San Jose Mercury News* followed one 1994 transaction involving a nearly new Lexus, worth $50,000 at the time, stolen in Los Gatos, for which Norman Kwan paid young thieves between $1,000 and $3,000. The car was stored in the San Gabriel garage of Victor Chan and Weidong Sun who cleaned and polished it, removed its license plates, and drove it to the Port of Los Angeles, into a waiting steel container, for its voyage to the People's Republic of China.[14]

The total cost to the exporters, including payment to the thieves, ocean freight, and modest bribes in Shanghai or Manchuria, approached $10,000. The fair market price of the Lexus in Shanghai or Beijing would be something like $170,000. Bousian estimated the exporters' profit margin to be $160,000.

The partners' income was considerably reduced in 1994 when the interagency Task Force for Regional Auto Theft Prevention intercepted twenty-one of their cars en route to China, including the Los Gatos Lexus, which was loaded by that time, and arrested Kwan, Sun, and Chan, along with two Chinese businessmen identified as buyers. Unfortunately for these five exporters, they lost a large shipment of cars and went to jail after several license plates and a list of serial numbers found in the San Gabriel garage helped identify them.[15]

It's the glitter and value of jewelry, however, that retains its lure among those of wealth and fame. Marvin Mitchelson is another example. Los Angeles attorney Marvin Mitchelson is perhaps best known as the inventor of palimony, a term which he introduced in the 1970s while representing Michelle Triola in her suit for financial support against movie actor Lee Marvin. Triola's palimony suit, although ultimately unsuccessful, deluged Mitchelson with favorable publicity, which *The New York Times* said "brought in newer and richer clients and made [Mitchelson] arguably the most famous lawyer in the world."[16]

In the late 1980s Mitchelson, who had been enjoying a decade of free-wheeling prosperity, began to have difficulties. The California State Bar accused him of overcharging clients and of failing to provide services to which he was committed; two California courts fined him $40,000 for frivolous appeals; six women accused him of rape; the Internal Revenue Service pursued him for over half a million dollars in delinquent taxes; and a number of creditors sued for nonpayment of debts, including the chief justice of the Bahamas Supreme Court, who placed a lien on Mitchelson's house.[17]

Nina Iliescu and Marvin Mitchelson

One of his more colorful credit problems arose in early April 1987 when he bid 1.4 million Swiss francs at a Sotheby's charity auction in Geneva for two ornate necklaces from the estate of the Duchess of Windsor. When Sotheby's had not been paid for the jewels some months later, they sued him in early 1989 for $1,215,000, including interest and lawyers' fees. Mitchelson said the delay in payment was because of a minor dispute over whether the bill would be paid in U.S. or Swiss currency, but Sotheby's, which never received full payment, got a court order in early 1990 placing Mitchelson's elegant nineteenth-floor law office in receivership. He had unloaded the necklaces, which Sotheby's recovered in London and sold for a third of what he had bid. Even though they gave him credit for this amount, he still owed them nearly a million dollars.[18]

Smuggling entered into the picture as well. Nina Iliescu, Mitchelson's companion on the trip to Geneva, said that when they flew back to California after the auction he carried the jewelry in his pants pocket, making no customs declaration. Although the State Bar prosecutor announced that she would charge him with smuggling, prosecutors ultimately found other charges more important and easier to document.[19]

In January 1993 Assistant U.S. Attorney Michael Reese appeared before Judge William Keller's U.S. District Court to charge Mitchelson with four felony counts of tax fraud, failure to report $2 million income in his tax returns from 1983 to 1986, false expense claims, and fraudulent deductions. Mitchelson filed for bankruptcy and unchivalrously blamed his tax problems on his accountant, who was called as a prosecution witness. To the prosecution's charge that Mitchelson "spent money like wildfire" the defense counsel replied that the defendant had a prosperous image to maintain. The jury found him guilty, and Judge Keller convicted him as charged. As he was led away in handcuffs, Mitchelson complained of chest pains and spent the next few days in a hospital rather than in jail. Judge Keller sentenced him, on April 12, to thirty months in prison and fined him $2 million for back taxes and interest. He appealed his conviction to the Ninth Circuit Court of Appeals and while the appeal was pending was free on bail for two years. The appeal was denied. His attorneys then appealed to the U.S. Supreme Court, also without success. Mitchelson began his prison term in November 1995.

A few weeks earlier his bank had sold his 9,000-square-foot house, called The Castle, to movie actor Johnny Depp. The Castle, originally built in 1922 and home during the 1930s to old-time spook star Bela Lugosi, brought $2.3 million, more than double what Mitchelson had paid in 1980. Anticipating the need for cash, he had put The Castle on the market in 1994, asking $9.9 million.[20]

Smuggling was of less importance in Marvin Mitchelson's fall from grace than some of his other differences with the federal government. Perhaps, on the other hand, if he had begun to pay Sotheby's for the Duchess's necklaces, no one would have asked Nina Iliescu how he carried them home.

Endnotes

1. *The New York Times* 10 January 1939, p. 1; 1 February 1939, p. 1; 23 March 1939, p. 21; and 9 May 1939, p. 1.

2. Ibid., 6 February 1947, pp. 1–2; and *San Francisco Chronicle* 7 February 1947, p. 1 ff.

3. *San Jose Mercury News* 7 February 1947, pp. 1–2.

4. *The New York Times* 15 April 1947, p. 2.

5. Ibid., 29 May 1947, p. 2.

6. *The New York Times* 17 July 1947, p. 9; and "General Court-Martial Orders No. 85," U.S. Department of the Army, 15 April 1948.

7. *The New York Times* 17 July 1947, p. 9; and "General Court-Martial Orders No. 85," U.S. Department of the Army, 15 April 1948.

8. *San Francisco Chronicle* 29 March 1949, p. 5.

9. *San Francisco Chronicle* 16 November 1948, p. 27; 29 March 1949, p. 5; and *Murray v. Lieutenant General Wedemeyer*, 21 F. 28431 (U.S. Dist. 1948).

10. *Murray v. Lieutenant General Wedemeyer*, 179 F. 2d 963 (9th Cir. Ct. 1949); and Department of Veterans' Administration Records Management Center, letter to author, 22 June 1996.

11. William M. Clements Library, *Eighteenth Century Documents Relating to the Royal Forests, the Sheriffs and Smuggling; Selected from the Shelbourne Manuscripts*, ed. Arthur Lyon Cross (New York: Macmillan, 1928), pp. 21–23.

12. William Noble, *Bookbanning in America* (Middlebury, VT: Paul S. Eriksson, 1990); and *The New York Times* 20 July 1998, sec. B, p. 1.

13. *San Francisco Chronicle* 14 September 1995, sec. A, p. 19.

14. *San Jose Mercury News* 1 September 1994, sec. B, p. 1.

15. Ibid.

16. *The New York Times* 4 April 1987, p. 16; and 1 July 1988, p. 10.

17. John A. Jenkins, *Ladies' Man; the Life and Trials of Marvin Mitchelson* (New York: St. Martin's Press, 1992), pp. 139–146.

18. Ibid., pp. 198–203; and *San Francisco Chronicle* 5 December 1988, sec. A, p. 10.

19. Jenkins, 200; *San Francisco Chronicle* 5 December 1988, sec. A, p. 10; and 30 June 1989, sec. A, p. 2.

20. *San Jose Mercury News* 6 February 1993, sec. A, p. 4; 9 February 1993, sec. B, p. 3; 10 February 1993, sec. A, p. 4; *San Francisco Chronicle* 10 February 1993, sec. A, p. 9; 13 April 1993, sec. A, p. 5; 30 March 1995, sec. A, p. 22; 1 November 1995, p. 8; and 5 December 1995, sec. A, p. 10.

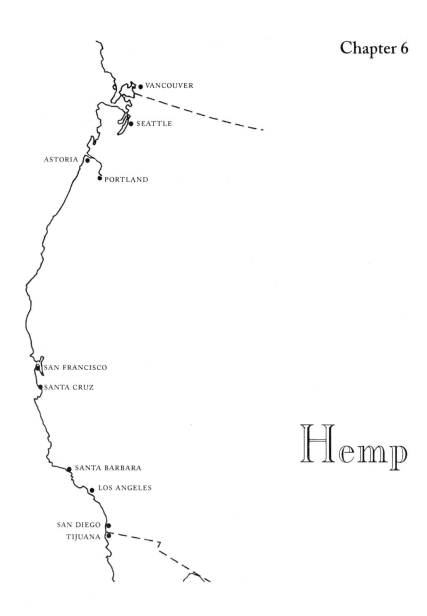

Chapter 6

Hemp

Patrick Hallinan had many friends and admirers in San Francisco where he was born, had lived for most of his life, and had practiced law as the senior partner of the firm of Hallinan, Poplack, and Levine since 1963. In 1974 he agreed to represent a client from Lake Tahoe who didn't fit the profile which Hallinan professed in the Martindale-Hubbell directory as "federal and state judges, public officials, attorneys, and corporations." Ciro Mancuso was a personable young man, a real estate developer and skier, whose principal interest at the time was the import and sale of marijuana. The Mancuso account was one which Hallinan lived to regret.

Mancuso and several of his skiing friends had been smuggling and distributing Mexican pot in the early 1970s when a southeast Asian acquaintance gave them a sample of a powerful Thai hemp with a retail value four times that of the Mexican weed. Their informant made the necessary introductions and therewith launched a new and richly rewarding import business.

Their first shipment, in 1976, recalled in a 1995 account in the *San Francisco Chronicle*, was in a travel trailer built with hollow wall spaces sufficient to hold 1,200 pounds of marijuana. The skiers had previously used a hollow-walled trailer very satisfactorily in getting pot across the Mexican border. The trailer was dispatched on shipboard to Thailand for an ostensible sightseeing trip. It returned in due course with its wall cavities full. They sold the shipment for $1.8 million. At the time they recognized, however, that trailer vacations to Thailand would eventually strike the authorities as somewhat out of the KOA circuit.[1]

In 1977 they invested $93,000 of their newly found wealth in a sturdy forty-foot ketch named the *Drifter*, shipped it to Singapore, and hired a Swiss sailor as captain of a three-man crew to load it and sail it back to California. The *Drifter* took three months to cross the Pacific, sailed in through the Golden Gate on June 2, 1977, and anchored on the north shore of San Pablo Bay, where skier-partner Jeff Welch unloaded its 2,200 pound cargo in sturdy rubber boats called Zodiacs, stored it in a rented space in Healdsburg, and arranged its distribution to retailers from Marin County to Nevada.

Everything went smoothly until the *Drifter*, en route to an East Bay boat yard, was stopped by a Richmond police launch, and a search revealed a twenty-eight-pound cache of marijuana under a cabin floorboard. The crew member who had been motoring the boat across the bay was arrested and was interviewed at some length. He was a cabinetmaker who had built secret compartments for the owners and had been one of three crewmen on the 7,000-mile voyage across the Pacific. During the course of his interrogation he revealed details of the skiers' import business which eventually interested federal agents, though he was the only one immediately indicted.

Sensing the threat of a serious problem, Mancuso went to San Francisco to get Patrick Hallinan's professional assistance. The crewman was freed on $50,000 bail and later recalled being chastised by Hallinan for being so garrulous. He eventually got off with three years' probation and 500 hours of community service. Since only a small amount of marijuana had been found aboard the *Drifter* (one customs agent was quoted as saying "What the heck! Twenty-eight pounds is a normal party in Marin"), Hallinan was able to divert the authorities from further prosecution. Mancuso later recalled that he wasn't even questioned at the time.[2]

The voyage of the *Drifter* netted the skiers more than $3 million, and they proceeded to expand their operations. Between 1977 and 1989 they landed at least sixteen increasingly substantial cargoes of Thai marijuana. Mancuso later reported that 1986 was their most successful year, with three landings, one at Gaviota and two in the Sacramento River delta, with a total value of more than $30 million. Federal authorities, however, were increasingly interested in their endeavors, and in 1987 and 1988 they lost four large cargoes, one in Australia and three on the coast of northern California and Oregon.

After the fifty-foot *California Sun* had made one successful 1986 landing in Oregon just north of the California border at Frankfort Beach, known as Smuggler's Cove during Prohibition, the Coast Guard was on the lookout. On the night of June 21, 1987, a man living above the cove, seeing a vessel close to shore with no running lights, called the sheriff, and the Coast Guard was there in no time. The *California Sun* tried to escape, was wrecked on the rocks, and lost its ten-ton cargo, and its crew and welcoming committee were apprehended. In the wreck of the *California Sun*, the pot importers not only lost a seaworthy fishing boat and a $22 million cargo but eventually suffered thirty-two convictions.

On October 25, 1989, Mancuso was arrested in his 10,000-square-foot mansion in the fashionable ski resort of Squaw Valley in the Sierra Nevada mountains and taken to Sacramento where he was jailed.

For five months, confined in Sacramento, Mancuso refused to betray his friends to improve his own uncomfortable position. However, federal agents had found and frozen $4 million in Mancuso's Swiss bank accounts and were building a strong case against him. Hallinan apparently negotiated an agreement with prosecutors in which Mancuso agreed to testify against his friends. In exchange for this cooperation the U.S. Attorney's office agreed not to indict his wife, Andrea, and to allow the Mancusos to keep a million dollars in European bank accounts and Squaw Valley property worth $3 million.[3]

In the summer of 1990 Hallinan fell from a ladder, broke his heel, and after surgery contracted pneumonia. During his convalescence he turned over the Mancuso case to an assistant, Katherine Alfieri. When Hallinan was able to return to the case, he discovered that his every-man-for-himself strategy had backfired. Mancuso, then jailed in Reno, informed him that henceforth Alfieri would represent him and dismissed Hallinan.

Mancuso and Alfieri persuaded Anthony White, assistant U.S. attorney in Reno, that Hallinan, a big-city lawyer who had been tutoring and abetting the Tahoe smugglers for eighteen years, was a more interesting target than Mancuso and his skiing friends, and they offered their active cooperation in building a criminal conspiracy case against him. Hallinan, along with eleven other defendants, was indicted at the beginning of August 1993 and faced the possibility of twenty years in jail. Hallinan, arrested at gunpoint in his Marin County home on August 4, spent five days in jail before his wife and law partner Lauren Poplack and his brother, San Francisco Supervisor Terrence Hallinan, posted $300,000 bail.[4]

He immediately engaged John Keker, a San Francisco attorney who had achieved prominence as special prosecutor of Iran-Contra defendant Oliver North, to represent him in the trial in the U.S. District Court in Reno. Keker's defense strategy was to muster strong character witnesses for Hallinan and to impugn the credibility of the prosecution's witnesses, repeatedly reminding the jury that most of them were convicted felons. It was a long battle, but on March 7, 1995, Hallinan was acquitted.[5]

On June 27, Judge Edward C. Reed of the U.S. District Court in Reno sentenced Mancuso to nine years in federal prison, in spite of defense counsel Alfieri's suggestion that her client was "a rehabilitated man" and that probation and community service were the appropriate sentences. Judge Reed did acknowledge that Mancuso had been exceptionally cooperative but reminded him that he had been responsible for the importation of 66,900 pounds of Thai marijuana, which he calculated as the equivalent of 59 million joints. In recognition of his cooperative attitude, Judge Reed gave him credit for the seventeen months he had spent in jail since his arrest in 1993 and allowed him two months to arrange his affairs before reporting to a federal penitentiary to begin his sentence.[6]

Although Mancuso and his fellow skiers amassed substantial wealth in the import business, another group of entrepreneurs, Dredge Master Associates, Inc., of Napa, with connections in Colombia, operated on an even grander scale, albeit briefly, during the late 1980s.

One of Mancuso's problems, in which he implicated Hallinan, was concealing the movement of money. Dredge Master solved this problem through a close family relationship with the Lendvest Mortgage Company of Napa, through which it was able to dissipate its drug income among many small bank deposits, thus evading the federal requirements that transactions of over $10,000 be explicitly reported.

Dredge Master Associates was incorporated in November 1984 and acquired a tug named *Ruby R*. In August 1987, after an air trip to Colombia, the skipper, Calvin Robinson, took the *Ruby R* to meet a larger vessel a thousand miles west of San Francisco, where he apparently picked up thirty tons of hashish and subsequently unloaded it on the Sacramento River delta.[7]

Dredge Master's marine and fiscal operations were both family affairs; its mailing address was the home of Calvin Robinson's sister, Sue Lemmons, near the Napa Country Club. Sue Lemmons's husband Don was appraiser and a board member of the Lendvest Mortgage Company. Envy of this familial relationship may have motivated an anonymous informant, outside the family circle, to suggest to the Napa police in 1987 that dredging was not Dredge Master's principal interest. The tip was relayed to Customs, the IRS, the DEA, and the Coast Guard.[8]

After the *Ruby R*'s successful trip, Robinson acquired a barge and a seventy-two-foot tug, the *Intrepid Venture*, which was registered to his sister, Diana Rauch. She, with Robinson and their sister Sue Lemmons, also deposited nearly a quarter of a million dollars in Napa bank accounts during the month of October 1987, presumably proceeds from sale of the *Ruby R*'s cargo.⁹

The barge and the *Intrepid Venture* were moored at Rio Vista on the Sacramento River delta where Calvin Robinson, his son, stepson, and two nephews spent three months rehabilitating them, equipping them, and preparing concealable compartments for cargo in the barge. These compartments were designed, welded, and painted so well that Coast Guardsmen found them only after drilling through a three-eights-inch steel plate.¹⁰

The Robinsons were apparently not acutely aware of a lone fisherman in a small dinghy nearby along the delta shore who was in fact Customs Agent Norman Wood. When the *Intrepid Venture* towed the barge out through the Golden Gate on May 6, the Coast Guard noted its departure, though it did not follow closely enough to observe the rendezvous. "We weren't able to catch the mother ship because we weren't quick enough," Coast Guard Admiral John D. Costello later admitted.¹¹

The Coast Guard cutter *Cape Romain* was on hand, however, to greet the *Intrepid Venture* as it came in through the Golden Gate at nine P.M. on May 23, bound for the Sacramento River. An armed boarding party of Coast Guardsmen and Customs agents who arrested the crew reported that "there was no resistance" and the suspect vessels were escorted to Yerba Buena Island.

Though customs agents had noticed a substantial amount of welding equipment aboard the barge, it was not until the next morning, after an all-night search, that Coast Guard officials found the hidden compartments. During the course of the day a large Coast Guard crew removed 1,500 fifty-pound burlap containers of hashish and 1,400 packages of Thai marijuana. A Coast Guard officer later reported that the barge was "top-notch shape." Customs agents were pleased with the fifteen tons of captured marijuana and announced that the thirty-seven and one-half tons of hash was "the largest hashish bust in U.S. history."[12] The amounts later reported in court records were forty-three tons of hashish and thirteen tons of marijuana.[13]

Calvin Robinson and six of his relatives were arrested at the end of May. He and the four members of his crew on the *Intrepid Venture* were indicted during the first week in June and his sisters and two other members of the Lendvest board on June 14. All but Robinson were released on bail the following day.[14]

Calvin Robinson, at his trial in February, suffered two disadvantages: previous convictions of burglary, forgery, and counterfeiting and his decision, as the jury was being selected, to plead his own defense. He was given somewhat reluctant permission by U.S. District Court Judge John Vukasin to act as his own defense counsel, having rejected the services of Paul Wolf, his court appointed attorney, who had refused, as frivolous, several of Robinson's defense suggestions.

The four crewmen of the *Intrepid Venture* wisely hired their own lawyers and asked for a separate trial, sensing that their captain was on a dangerous course. Thanks to skillful defense counsel, which managed to persuade the jury that the crewmen who had loaded and concealed the huge cargo of cannabis products were unaware of what they were transporting, all the Robinsons except Calvin were eventually acquitted.[15]

Robinson, a tall and substantially built figure, had assembled six boxes and three bags of documents on which to base his defense, condensed into one box at the Court's insistence, and argued his innocence with imagination and enthusiasm, saying that "the government's hands are dirty; my hands are clean" and defending the cruise of the *Intrepid Venture*. "We were working men on the water," he said. "We ran a boat and we towed a barge."[16]

He further asserted that he was the victim of "a perversional law which encourages our public representatives to plunder our lives" and that he was the target of "Eliot Nesses of the 1980s, like Ed Meese" (Attorney General, 1985–88). Responding to his exceptional self-confidence and the inventiveness of his defense, as well as a prickly demeanor which occasionally verged on contempt of court, the jury, on February 22, 1989, found him guilty on six counts of drug smuggling and conspiracy. On June 8 Judge Vukasin sentenced him to life in prison without parole and a fine of $4 million.[17]

The Lemmonses and others charged with concealing deposits of drug money got off scot-free, except for David Hanson, former president of Lendvest, and Robert Pitner, owner of a Napa Valley winery. Both were convicted of money laundering.[18]

In August 14, 1990, Calvin Robinson appealed his sentence to the Ninth Circuit Court in San Francisco, asserting that he had been denied proper counsel both in conviction and sentencing. The appellate court denied the appeal of conviction but remanded the case to the District Court because he had asked for, and been denied (the appellate court decided, inappropriately), counsel at sentencing.[19] Judge Vukasin saw no reason to reduce his sentence and, in fact, in the retrial on June 25 specified that he serve it in a maximum security prison and be charged $1,200 per month for costs.[20]

Endnotes

1. *San Francisco Chronicle* 18 January 1995, sec. A, p. 1.

2. Ibid.

3. *Los Angeles Times* 6 March 1995, sec. A, p. 1 ff.

4. *San Francisco Chronicle* 10 August 1993, sec. A, p. 1.

5. Ibid.

6. Ibid., 28 June 1995, sec. A, pp. 13, 16.

7. Ibid., 29 June 1988, sec. A, p. 8.

8. Ibid., 25 May 1988, sec. A, p. 1.

9. Ibid., 15 June 1988, sec. A, p. 2.

10. Ibid., 25 May 1988, sec. A, pp. 1, 6.

11. Ibid.; and 8 November 1988, sec. A, p. 4.

12. *San Francisco Chronicle* 25 May 1988, sec. A, pp. 1, 6; and 8 November 1988, sec. A, p. 4.

13. *San Francisco Chronicle* 15 June 1988, sec. A, p. 2; and 16 June 1988, sec. A, p. 30; and *United States v. Calvin Lyniol Robinson*, 913 F. 2d 713 (U.S. Dist. 1989).

14. *San Francisco Chronicle* 15 June 1988, sec. A, p. 2; and 16 June 1988, sec. A, p. 30; and *United States v. Calvin Lyniol Robinson*, 913 F. 2d 713 (U.S. Dist. 1989).

15. *San Francisco Chronicle* 23 February 1989, sec. A, p. 3.

16. Ibid., 7 February 1989, sec. A, p. 8.

17. *San Jose Mercury News* 9 June 1989, sec. F, p. 1.

18. *San Francisco Chronicle* 15 June 1989, sec. A, p. 12.

19. *United States v. Calvin Lyniol Robinson*, 718.

20. *San Francisco Chronicle* 26 June 1992, sec. A, p. 20.

Chapter 7

Illegal Immigrants

n July 1995, south of Hawaii, the U.S. Coast Guard boarded the *Jung Sheng No. 8*, of Panamanian registry, and escorted it to Honolulu. There were 147 Chinese passengers aboard, bound for the west coast of North America, more than thirty of them ill from dehydration. Several reported physical and psychological abuse by the smuggling gang's "enforcers," whom they accused of repeatedly beating them and making them sign IOUs with their own blood. There were seven women among the passengers, and interestingly they did not complain of abuse. A State Department representative assigned to the incident told a *Newsday* reporter that the Taiwanese captain and one crew member were returned to Taiwan; nine crew members, eighteen enforcers, and all the passengers were repatriated to China.[1]

There have been millions of Chinese immigrants to America during the course of the last century. However, there is evidence that Chinese migration to California began over a millennium earlier. Chinese ships may have reached the American West Coast, which they called *Fu-sang*, as early as the fifth century A.D. Most Chinese immigrants to California in the nineteenth century, according to historian Sandy Lydon in *Chinese Gold, the Chinese in the Monterey Bay Region*, came from Kwangtung province, many of them refugees from poverty and civil strife. When reports of Sutter's gold reached Hong Kong in 1849, there was a predictable response in southern China. Tens of thousands of able-bodied men who could afford passage boarded ships for *Gum Shan* (the Golden Mountain).[2]

Chinese Immigrant

In the gold fields the Chinese were moderately successful, in spite of race prejudice and exploitation. In the 1860s they were actually encouraged to come to America to work on construction of the transcontinental railroads. Thousands responded, and hundreds perished in the rough and dangerous business of laying tracks across the desert and the Sierra Nevada mountains. Lydon recalls that "when the Central Pacific and the Union Pacific Railroads joined in Utah in 1869, the Central Pacific released an estimated five thousand Chinese railroad workers."[3]

The economic decline of the early 1870s produced high unemployment in California, and because Chinese immigrants were thrifty, industrious, and willing to work for what the gold-rush mentality regarded as slave wages, there was widespread resentment among the Occidental immigrants, and particularly in San Francisco, the Chinese were frequently abused. The climax of this Sinophobia was the Chinese Exclusion Act of 1882.[4]

Chinese dreams of the Golden Mountain persisted, however, in spite of growing persecution. Asian immigrants disembarking at the Pacific Mail Steamship Company pier faced a long and painful ordeal of interrogation and confinement at the immigration station on Angel Island. From 1890 to 1920 the annual rate of Chinese immigration was reduced from thousands to hundreds.[5]

It was no wonder then that some of the more enterprising seekers of the Golden Mountain took ships to Mexico or Canada, from which they were able to make their way in small craft to Chinese coastal communities, where they could land at night and avoid San Francisco's hostile formalities. Lydon recalls that "the rocky coastline around Point Lobos offered good places to land Chinese immigrants smuggled in from Mexico and Canada" and that "during an 1892 smuggling incident involving the ship *Halcyon*, nineteen Chinese were landed at night at

Stillwater Cove, and several of them took refuge in a fisherman's shanty at Point Lobos before finally being captured by the sheriff."[6]

One victim of the Sinophobia prevailing in 1895 was Yee Kee, a Chinese resident of Brooklyn, the Chinese suburb across the Pajaro River from Watsonville, who that year returned to the old country to visit his family and to bring back a small stone religious statue for the Brooklyn shrine. The Chinese Exclusion Act was being assiduously enforced, and before leaving he sought assurance from John T. Porter, president of the Pajaro Valley Bank and owner of the Brooklyn area, that he would be able to reenter California. Porter was sure that he would be able to arrange it. When Yee returned in September 1895, aboard the steamer *Gaelic*, he was met by Porter's son Warren, who presented the authorities with a certificate of Yee's admissibility and escorted him back to Brooklyn. The certificate, signed by the elder Porter, another bank president, and the chairman of the Watsonville city council, identified Yee as a Watsonville merchant in good standing. Although merchants were admissible, Chinese laundrymen, who were classified as laborers, were not. Shortly a representative of the Immigration Service took Yee Kee back to San Francisco, having discovered that he had had a laundry as well as a store, and after a protracted hearing in which Watsonville's postmaster testified against him, Yee Kee was summarily deported.[7]

Many refugees from the Exclusion Act came across the long and lightly guarded Mexican border. In 1908 a man named Chin Bow testified that an Ensenada entrepreneur named Charlie Sam and three other men had charged him $310 to convey him across the line from Sonora to Imperial Junction.[8]

For the first half of the twentieth century the rate of Chinese immigration was low by comparison with that in the late nineteenth and in the years since World War II. However, the Yellow

Peril fixation of the 1870s faded as the economy improved and expanded, and although immigration quotas continued, prosperous Chinatowns developed in several California towns and cities. Chinese businessmen prospered, frequently sharing their wealth with relatives in China, and once again dreams of the Golden Mountain loomed in Chinese folklore.

After World War II the Exclusion Act was repealed. The 1968 Immigration and Nationality Act established national quotas of 20,000. By 1976 the number of immigrants from China, Hong Kong, and Taiwan was estimated to be more than 40,000 per year, the increase due to the fact that since 1950 more than half of all Chinese immigrants have entered as relatives of residents, exempting them from quotas.[9]

After the death of Mao Tse-tung in 1976 authoritarian control of China's economy was relaxed somewhat, and Taiwanese and overseas Chinese entrepreneurs were attracted to smuggling, both by air and by sea, as a good source of income. Although such contraband commodities as pirated CDs and computer software, parts of endangered animals, drugs, and jewelry were profitable, the transportation of undocumented Asian emigrants was for some time the favorite. Smugglers discovered that the penalties for being caught conveying illegal Chinese emigrants to Australia, Europe, and America were much less than those for transporting cocaine, bootleg CDs, or other goods and that the migrants would pay good money and accept indentured servitude to reach the Golden Mountain.

In a 1993 series of articles in the *San Francisco Chronicle*, Chinese-speaking reporter Pamela Burdman wrote a detailed account of the new tide of smuggled immigrants, most of them from Fujian province in southern China. Although she found customs authorities more concerned about the numbers of illegal immigrants arriving by air at New York, Los Angeles, and

San Francisco airports than those arriving by sea, the appearance of big shiploads of illegals found off the Pacific coast was more dramatic than the arrival of a few at a time by air.[10]

The smuggling of Chinese emigrants either by air or by sea required substantial capital and complex international networks. The smugglers' organizations were generally based on powerful associations of overseas Chinese like the Wo Hop To, of Taiwan and San Francisco, which reached not only across the Pacific but also were reported to be invading the territory of the Italian Mafia in Rome and its American families in New York and Latin America.[11]

Burdman's 1993 articles were timely. Shortly before dawn on the morning of May 24 of that year, the *Pai Sheng*, of Honduran registry, with Panamanian owners and a Taiwanese captain and crew, deposited some 250 undocumented Chinese immigrants on an old pier at Fort Point, under the south end of the Golden Gate Bridge. The exact number is unknown because a good many escaped in cars and on foot before the arrival of National Park police and agents of the Immigration and Naturalization Service (INS). The *Pai Sheng* was shortly captured and taken to Treasure Island.[12]

The number of illegal Chinese immigrants to California increased dramatically during the late 1980s, partly because of the Beijing government's suppression of dissidents most dramatically demonstrated in Tiananmen Square in 1989.

Another important factor in the increase was the United States Refugee Act, which came into effect April 1, 1980, that permitted most undocumented immigrants who had managed to set foot on American soil to apply for asylum as political refugees. If asylum was initially denied, the immigrants could appeal the denial and be given a temporary work permit while the appeal was being considered.

Smugglers and their clients depended on the fact that the appeal process might take several years. While the wheels of justice were slowly turning, it was difficult to keep track of the appellants, who had a strong tendency to disappear. Further, the more appeals that were pending, the slower the process. In effect, an illegal immigrant who could get to the United States might, with a little luck, stay indefinitely. By 1993 Fujianese immigrants were paying $25,000 to $30,000 each to "snakeheads," as the smugglers' recruiters were called, to transport them to Europe or America. Burdman estimated the gross income of the smuggling rings at that time to be three billion dollars per year. The INS was overwhelmed by the sheer volume of immigrant smuggling.[13]

In February 1992 three men paid $70,000 in cash at the Marina Village Yacht Harbor in Alameda for a fifty-seven-foot motor launch named the *Liberated Lady*. In less than a week, working day and night, they installed new electronic equipment and supplies. When they put to sea, the Coast Guard followed, interested in the manner of acquisition and of outfitting the *Liberated Lady*. After it had met an old freighter named the *Jinn Yin* off the coast of southern California, the Coast Guard boarded it and found eighty-five Chinese crowded into the cabin. Thirteen crew members of both vessels were jailed briefly, and their passengers applied for asylum.

In December 1992 the Coast Guard picked up the *Manyoshi Maru* off the coast of central California and escorted it to Treasure Island, where 171 illegal Chinese immigrants disembarked. In early February the Coast Guard replied to a distress signal from the *East Wood* near the Marshall Islands in the south Pacific. Aboard the crippled ship were 524 Chinese passengers, a record cargo.

After the May 24, 1993, landing of the *Pai Sheng* at Fort Point, little more than a week elapsed before two fishing boats based in Monterey Bay deposited 250 more Fujianese passengers early in the morning of Wednesday, June 2, at small-craft harbors south of San Francisco. At six A.M. the larger of the two, the sixty-foot *Angel*, landed 180 Chinese immigrants at Moss Landing on Monterey Bay, including ten women. At nine thirty the forty-six-foot *Pelican* was landing another hundred at Pillar Point. The *Angel*'s captain, Lung Van Nguyen, three Vietnamese *Pelican* crewmen, and Wing Wu, who made arrangements for land transportation, were arrested, as were members of a network headed by Wei Hing Lee, also known as White Tiger Lee, of Queens, New York.[14]

The magnitude of the problem posed by these operations for the INS and the Coast Guard was the source of considerable alarm in Washington in 1993, particularly in view of recent experience with the 1980 Refugee Act and the growing conviction in the INS that the only way to discourage the smuggling of undocumented migrants was to return the victims promptly to their places of origin.[15]

Therefore, when the Coast Guard received reports in early July of three rusty and uncommunicative ships off the coast of Baja California, they sent cutters to observe them. After ascertaining that the three ships, the *Long Sen 1*, the *Sing Lee 6*, and the *To Ching 212* were Taiwanese, and obtaining Taiwanese permission to apprehend them, members of one Coast Guard crew boarded the largest of the three, the 160-foot *Long Sen*, which had asked for help with an ailing engine.[16]

Finding that it had 236 Chinese passengers aboard, the Coast Guard received permission to board the other two ships. The total passenger count rose to 659. All the passengers appeared to be in good health, but there was a hurricane approaching from the south and all three ships were running low on food. Washington pressed the Mexican government to land the migrants and, since Mexico had no constraints comparable to those of the 1980 Refugee Act, to fly them back to China.

Mexico first refused, then, after a month's diplomatic pressure, to which current trade negotiations were apparently linked, Mexico acquiesced. Mexican officials pressed for review of migrants' questionnaires by representatives of the United Nations High Commission on Refugees but finally announced that they would prosecute the smugglers under Mexican law. The three vessels landed at Ensenada, and the passengers, under heavy security, were transported to the Tijuana airport where they boarded chartered aircraft for south China. U.N. representatives interviewed fifty-eight applicants for U.S. refugee status but only one was approved.[17]

Although the prompt return of 658 emigrants to China had a chilling effect on a formidable 1993 wave of snakehead clientele, the traffic continued, probing lines of least resistance in western Europe and North America. The 180-foot Taiwanese freighter *Jin Yinn No. 1*, thought to be the mother ship from which the *Angel* and the *Pelican* were loaded in June 1993, reappeared off the coast of Baja California in early April 1994, was apprehended with 121 Chinese passengers by Coast Guard cutters *Active* and *Sherman*, and was escorted to Guatemala.[18]

The Washington Post reported that summer that countries of eastern Europe, particularly Russia, were hosts to large numbers of Chinese migrants, ultimately headed for America and western Europe. He estimated that there were 60,000 of them at that time living illegally in Moscow.[19]

In the spring of 1995 two Taiwanese fishing boats, the *Fang Ming* and the *Xin Ji Li Hou* were apprehended off the west coast of Mexico by the U.S. Coast Guard. The *Fang Ming*, which had 106 passengers, was prevented by a Mexican navy vessel from landing on the west coast of Baja California, just south of the

California border, in late March. It was boarded by the U.S. Coast Guard on March 24 and eventually escorted by the navy to the port of San Carlos, where the passengers were received and interviewed by Mexican immigration officials. The *Xin Ji Li Hou*, with 150 passengers, boarded by the Coast Guard in mid-April, received similar treatment.[20]

The number of undocumented Asian immigrants crossing the southern border is minuscule in comparison with the tide of Mexicans and Central Americans who enter California by wading the turbid Tijuana River or braving the summer heat of the southwestern desert. The "levee gangs" or "coyotes," who exact a high price for transportation, tortillas, and travel advice, do in fact manage to get large numbers of their clients, including an occasional Asian, across, along with profitable quantities of cocaine, but abuse, neglect, and mortal danger are an integral part of their stock in trade.[21]

Because of the INS' difficulty in preventing undocumented immigrants from crossing the southwestern borders, there are undoubtedly snakehead ships still landing their clients on the west coast of Mexico, from which they travel north to an uncertain future. The clients pay dearly for this trip, during which they are frequently abused, and gamble desperately with their future. If they are successful, they may eventually own restaurants or importing businesses of their own. If the gods do not favor them, they are captured and returned home, deeply in debt, with nothing to show for it.

Endnotes

1. *San Francisco Chronicle* 23 August 1995, sec. A, p. 4.

2. Sandy Lydon, *Chinese Gold: the Chinese in the Monterey Bay Region* (Capitola, CA: Capitola Book Co., 1984), pp. 20–21; and Charles E. Chapman, *A History of California; the Spanish Period* (New York: Macmillan, 1930), pp. 23–30.

3. Lydon, p. 79.

4. Ibid.

5. *San Francisco Chronicle* 30 April 1993, sec. A, p. 16.

6. Lydon, pp. 140–141.

7. *Santa Cruz Sentinel* 12 October 1895, p. 3; and 19 October 1895, p. 1; *Santa Cruz Surf* 12 October 1895, p. 2; and *Watsonville Register-Pajaronian* 10 October 1895, p. 3; 17 October 1895, p. 3; and 29 October 1895, p. 3.

8. *San Francisco Chronicle* 19 December 1908, p. 3.

9. Ibid., 30 April 1993, sec. A, p. 16.

10. Ibid., 10 June 1993, sec. A, p. 1.

11. Ibid., 15 March 1995, sec. A, p. 12.

12. Ibid., 27–30 April 1993; 27–29 May 1993; and 13 December 1993.

13. *San Francisco Chronicle* 27 April 1993, sec. A, p. 1 ff.

14. U.S. Coast Guard, Monterey Group, unclassified dispatches, received 2 and 3 June 1993; *San Francisco Chronicle* 25 June 1993, p. 1; *Santa Cruz Sentinel* 3 June 1993, p. 1; and *Watsonville Register-Pajaronian* 3 June 1993, p. 1 ff.

15. *San Francisco Chronicle* 27 April 1993, sec. A, p. 1; 28 April 1993, sec. A, p. 1; and 10 July 1993, sec. A, p. 3.

16. *San Francisco Chronicle* 7 July 1993, sec. A, p. 4; and 8 July 1993, sec. A, p. 1.

17. *San Francisco Chronicle* 17 July 1993, sec. A, p. 1.

18. *San Jose Mercury News* 10 June 1994, sec. B, p. 3.

19. Ibid., 2 June 1994, sec. A, p. 1.

20. Ibid., 29 March 1995, sec. B, p. 4; and 20 April 1995, sec. B, p. 11.

21. Venson C. Davis, *Blood on the Border: Criminal Behavior and Illegal Immigration along the Southern U.S. Border* (New York: Vantage Press, 1991), p. 49 ff.

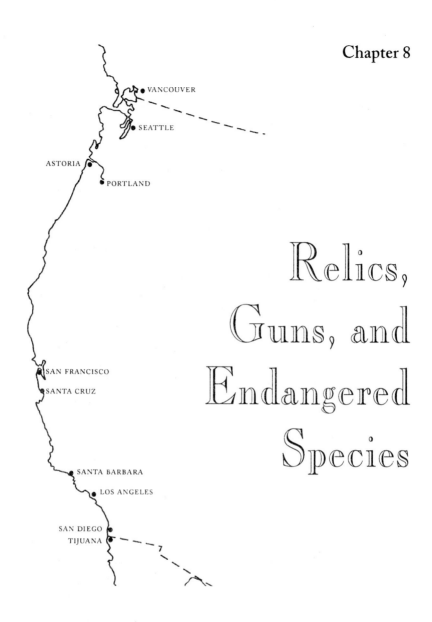

Chapter 8

Relics, Guns, and Endangered Species

H e had died young, still in his early thirties. He was
buried in his gold crown and ceremonial robes, in a
hardwood coffin. In his hand he held a ritual knife.
Beside him were his shield, a mask, bells, and ornate jewelry, all
of gold, and around him other symbols of his wealth and power

as a ruler of the Moche people. Nine members of his family and court were buried in the same low adobe pyramid.

The Moche flourished 1,500 years ago, a thousand years before the time of Inca dominance, on the coast of what is now northern Peru. This burial, in the opinion of University of California anthropologist Christopher B. Donnan, "far surpasses in the quantity of precious objects and the overall quality of the craftsmanship anything that we have ever seen that has come from scientific excavations."[1]

Professor Donnan and Walter Alva, director of the Bruning Museum in the regional capital of Lambayeque, who opened this remarkable tomb near the coastal village of Sipán, said the central figure of this burial was a warrior-priest. Wilbur Garrett, editor of *National Geographic*, which sponsored the excavation, called him a Peruvian King Tut. Alva discovered the grave under a shallow depression near other burial sites which had been recently looted. In this region of Peru plunder of ancient graves had in recent years become a basic industry. Alva hired an armed guard to protect his new excavation from enterprising grave robbers who made their living selling Moche relics to dealers in pre-Columbian art as well as tolerable copies to tourists.[2]

Alva and Donnan worked with professional care in opening the tomb of the warrior priest. Its contents were carefully recorded and moved to the Bruning Museum, with thirty pieces, insured for half a million dollars, lent to the National Geographic Society for display at its Washington D.C. headquarters.

Beautiful specimens of the Moche gold, jewelry, and ceramics dug from the tombs of Sipán had for some time been appearing in the hands of dealers and private collectors in North America and Europe. One California dealer had imported sufficient numbers of Sipán antiquities to attract the attention of United States Customs and Peruvian authorities.

In March 1988 Customs agents raided David Swetnam's art gallery in Santa Barbara and the homes of two other dealers and several southern California collectors, confiscating 1,300 pre-Columbian art objects, many of them thought to have come from Sipán.

Swetnam and his wife Jacquelyn were the first indicted for criminal conspiracy and fraudulent customs declarations. Swetnam was the only one of the suspects convicted and that on the only charge to which he pleaded guilty, in a plea bargain to spare his wife, of customs fraud, for which he eventually spent six months in federal prison. One of the other dealers, Benjamin Johnson, former conservator of the Los Angeles County Art Museum, acquitted of charges of receiving stolen goods, was ably defended by Professor John Henry Merryman of the Stanford Law School, who argued that reputable art dealers should not be penalized for Peru's failure to protect its cultural patrimony. Johnson's vindication was a great relief to him, to Swetnam, and to their fellow art dealers. Only a few pieces were returned to Peru, all from Swetnam's collection. One of the other collectors, a Nobel laureate professor from the California Institute of Technology, was reported to be negotiating the voluntary return of additional pieces in his possession. Nevertheless, the market for Moche antiquities remained bullish.[3]

The lure of Peruvian gold from ancient ruins appeals to a limited market. An item affording greater opportunities for smugglers were guns.

Americans' infatuation with guns, nurtured by Second-Amendment mantras of the National Rifle Association, had in the early 1980s attracted the attention of Chinese entrepreneurs eager for new U.S. markets. The demand for assault weapons easily converted from semi-automatic to machine guns seemed particularly promising. The fact that importing assault weapons had just been prohibited by the Bush Administration confirmed them as street weapons of choice and encouraged, rather than intimidated, the smugglers.[4]

By the summer of 1989, after Patrick Edward Purdy's Stockton schoolyard massacre using an AK-47, the U.S. Bureau of Alcohol, Tobacco, and Firearms (BATF) revealed that his was but one of tens of thousands of these Chinese assault rifles being smuggled into West Coast ports. Assault rifles were easily and abundantly available to gangs and drug dealers; their abundance brought prices as low as $258, well below the prevailing market.[5]

AK-47 Assault Rifle

Although customs officials were painfully aware of this deadly traffic, inspectors at the Port of Los Angeles, dealing with 75,000 incoming containers every month, reported that they could thoroughly inspect only one in fifty. They did announce that they were adding guns to their high priority list, along with heroin and cocaine.

By 1989 BATF agents had identified two AK-47 suppliers with close ties to the Chinese government: the China North Industries Corporation (Norinco) of Dalian, northern China, and Poly Technologies, an agency of the People's Liberation Army known to the trade as Polytech. They reported that many of these weapons, adapted from a sturdy Soviet army weapon designed by Mikhail Kalashnikov after World War II, had identical serial numbers and were stamped "56S." Many of the markings required by BATF were missing.

Hammond H. Ku, a 49-year-old Taiwanese resident of Saratoga, California, had been co-owner with his wife Sophia of a Mountain View restaurant which he sold to capitalize his weapons import business. His sister, Linda Huang of Atherton, was a travel agent, specializing in East Asia.

Richard Chen and his wife Ching Hua Chen were owners of restaurants in Soquel and Carmel, had access to warehouse space in the Santa Cruz area, and were friends of Ku and Huang. During the early 1990s, they were persuaded — apparently by the enterprising Mr. Ku — to supplement their other income by importing Chinese guns for the the drug-gang and private-militia markets. Richard Chen was reported to have connections with Norinco, which produced a large assortment of military weapons.

Ku, in his exploration of the American gun market, became acquainted with two high rollers who told him they had Miami Mafia connections, who didn't haggle about prices, who promptly produced a $400,000 down payment in cash, and who offered assistance in getting gun shipments through Customs. Ku assured them of the reliability of his high-level connections with the Chinese government and modestly asserted that he could on short notice supply not only 300,000 AK-47s but also tanks, machine guns with silencers, and anti-aircraft missiles called Red Parakeets, which Ku said would "bring down a jumbo jet."[6]

On March 18 the big shipment arrived in California, on the *Empress Phoenix*. Two thousand fully automatic AK-47s, packed in boxes in a large container, were unloaded in the Port of Oakland. The two high-rolling mafiosi, one a BATF agent, the other from the Customs Service, had seven smugglers ripe for arrest. Although they had also hoped to pick up two Norinco executives whom Ku said he had invited to California and Robert Ma of Los Altos, an elusive weapons dealer who was abroad at the time, they became concerned that news of their sting operation would leak to the press, so they made their move, confiscating the guns and arresting co-conspirators Ku, Huang, the Chens, and two men who were experts at converting semi-automatic weapons to rapid-fire. Ma prudently remained abroad, presumably in China.[7]

The indictment of the smugglers had diplomatic implications since Norinco and Poly Technologies were both Chinese government factories, but the Department of State, with the disk piracy and other weapons export problems already creating tension at the China desk, blandly asked the Chinese embassy to help find the culprits and to discourage further shipments, which seemed likely to continue. Prosecution promised to move slowly, and the suspects were all released on bail, set for both Ku and Chen at a million dollars each.[8]

Although the urban American gun market is flourishing, high demand in the Philippines has caused smugglers to divert some of California's abundance to Manila, where prohibitive gun laws adopted during the Marcos regime have for twenty years guaranteed premium prices for smuggled handguns and ammunition.

It was ammunition — 356 pounds of smokeless powder in sixty-pound cannisters wrapped in aluminum foil, a lethal cargo found on June 9, 1987 aboard a China Airlines 747 about to leave San Francisco for Manila — which alerted the Customs Service to the growing American export of guns to the Philippines. A Daly City family, Rafael David, his wife Grace, and his sisters Leila and Leonila, had bought and packed the gunpowder, wrapping the packages in clothing. When they were arrested on June 18, 1987, federal agents also found 20,000 primers for pistol ammunition in their Daly City house.[9]

Rollin Klink, special agent in charge of the Customs Service investigation, described the Davids' shipment as part of a growing Philippine-American cottage industry with its beginnings in 1972, when then-President Ferdinand Marcos prohibited private gun ownership. Nick Benoza, a Philippine-American journalist in San Francisco, said that recent gun shipments to Manila had been entirely profit-driven, whereas a 1981 shipment of explosives by Steve Psinakis, then of San Francisco, was designed to facilitate the overthrow of Ferdinand Marcos in 1986. Benoza estimated the 1987 street price of guns in Manila at three to five times their cost in California. People were willing to pay these high Manila prices for personal security, he said, because of insurgency in the Philippines. Klink was particularly concerned at the safety hazard posed by air shipments of gunpowder.[10]

Richard Dean Pedrioli of Modesto was arrested on August 29, 1989, for shipping seventy guns to Manila in boxes labeled as auto parts. The shipment was escorted by courier Dominique Adams, who identified herself as a model and resident of Salt Lake City. Adams, when she was apprehended in Manila, said she didn't know what was in the boxes, and when Pedrioli testified that he had deceived her, she was eventually released. Pedrioli, who had been arrested in 1988 for sending guns to Manila, was sentenced to five years and four months in prison on November 20, 1989.[11]

Guns are not everyone's forte, so there are types of contraband to suit all tastes.

William Baumgartl, M.D., of Oakland was president in 1994 of the Bay Area Carnivorous Plant Society, an organization devoted to collection and propagation of the 600 known species of carnivorous plants. The Society had grown, during its first five years, to a membership of 200. An anesthesiologist by profession and a committed collector, Baumgartl remodeled his home to accommodate his exotic flora and turned his garage into a sophisticated plant-propagation laboratory.

It was on a collecting expedition in pursuit of rare southeast Asian pitcher plants that he flew to Indonesia in September 1994 with his friends Eric von Geldern, an Alameda County deputy district attorney, and Curtis Tom, a Mountain View businessman.

They were successful in their jungle search for the carnivorous pitcher plants of the *Nepenthaceae* family, of which they brought 200 specimens home, some in their hand luggage and some in boxes with customs forms attached saying that the contents were "T-shirts and trinkets." They knew that their prizes violated the Convention on International Trade in Endangered Species of Wild Fauna and Flora. Still, previous U.S. enforcement of the Endangered Species Act had been sporadic and penalties light. The three collectors felt that the specimens they had collected were worth the risk.[12]

Before returning home they mailed many of their 200 plants. Suspicious customs inspectors intercepted most of their packages, and when their contents had been identified, Baumgartl, von Geldern, and Tom were arrested, charged with smuggling endangered plants, and released on bail.

At their trial in April 1995 in federal court in Los Angeles, their attorneys, arguing that by collecting the plants the defendants were probably rescuing them from endangered habitats, managed a plea bargain in which each of them agreed to pay a $10,000 fine and perform 200 hours of community service.[13]

Meat-eating plants were not the only botanical contraband to get smugglers in trouble that year. In November a twenty-eight-year-old Indonesian named Harto Kolopaking, son of a prominent nurseryman in Java, pleaded guilty to charges that during the preceding two years he had smuggled over 1,300 rare lady's slipper orchids into northern California.[14]

Lady's Slipper Orchid

The species of lady's slippers in question, known to botanists as *Paphiopedilum*, grow wild in Java, and are, like pitcher plants, on the endangered species list. Although previous violations had brought smugglers nothing worse than probation and fines, Kolopaking's offense was prosecuted as a felony, and he received a five-month prison sentence. The federal prosecutor, who had asked for sixteen months, said this severe sentence was because of the large number of orchids which Kolopaking had shipped. The government's estimate increased during the trial from 1,346 to 1,500.[15]

One of the more exotic imports of rare and endangered species was revealed in January 1985 when customs agents in San Francisco noticed that a package arriving from Australia was expanding and contracting in a way that caused them to report that "the package was breathing."[16] Special Agent Scott Pearson of the U.S. Fish and Wildlife Service assisted in opening the package, in which they found a live, six-foot python. The package was addressed to Robert Stene, at his father's home in San Jose. Federal agents confiscated the python and began a close watch of the Stene house.

Robert Stene and David Rittenhouse traveled frequently to Australia and Mexico, where at very little cost they acquired exotic reptiles such as snakes, lizards, skinks, chameleons, monitors, turtles, and tortoises, many of them endangered species and therefore illegally caught and shipped from their habitat to California. Australian specimens had either to be shipped by air, carefully packed in small boxes, or carried in hand luggage. Mexican reptiles were either carried in luggage or hidden in auto door panels or other inconspicuous vehicle spaces. Government agents built their case slowly over a two-year period during which they confiscated more than ninety reptiles, most of which had survived. The estimated fifteen percent which had died were frozen as evidence.[17]

On June 4, 1987, Stene was arrested, and U.S. Attorney Joseph Russoniello filed a twenty-seven-count indictment against him and Rittenhouse, naming four other San Jose youths as co-defendants. They also searched the Stene house, which George Elkins of the Fish and Wildlife Service described to the *San Jose Mercury News.*

> Both bathrooms were filled from floor to ceiling with boxes of snakes, and in the back yard there were huge African tortoises. Plus, there were forty-eight cages scattered around, and half of those were filled with reptiles. In the basement were cages filled with mice and pinkies — those are the baby mice that are used to feed the reptiles.[18]

Elkins, noting that at the time of the raid most of the reptiles were legal, said, "It looked like the place had been cleaned out by the time we got there." He guessed that Stene and Rittenhouse, aware that quite a few of their illegal shipments were not arriving, suspected that they were being confiscated and that their business was in trouble.[19]

In 1994, a stiff jail sentence went to the unfortunate Stephen E. Cook, a Los Angeles dealer in exotic reptiles and insects who, when he was arrested, had imported over 600 rare red-kneed tarantulas from Colima, Mexico. Cook had paid three dollars each for the big spiders, an endangered species both in Mexico and the United States, smuggled them across the border in his personal luggage, and sold them to collectors for as much as forty-five dollars each. The transaction which caused his downfall was an attempt to sell 215 imported tarantulas to an agent of the Arizona Fish and Game Department. On November 7, 1994, Cook was sentenced to eight years in prison.[20]

Endnotes

1. *San Francisco Chronicle* 14 September 1988, sec. A, p. 1.

2. *Los Angeles Times* 14 September 1988, p. 1; and 12 October 1989, sec. A, p. 3.

3. *Los Angeles Times* 13 October 1989, sec. A, p. 3.

4. *San Jose Mercury News* 9 May 1989, sec. A, p. 6.

5. Ibid.; and *The Washington Post* 5 July 1989, sec. A, p. 13.

6. *Los Angeles Times* 24 May 1996, sec. A, p. 1; and *San Jose Mercury News* 24 May 1996, p. 1.

7. *Los Angeles Times* 24 May 1996, sec. A, p. 1; and *San Jose Mercury News* 24 May 1996, p. 1.

8. *The Washington Post* 25 May 1996, sec. A, p. 6.

9. *San Francisco Chronicle* 24 June 1987, p. 8.

10. *San Jose Mercury News* 20 June 1987, sec. B, p. 1.

11. *San Francisco Chronicle* 31 August 1989, sec. A, p. 28; and *Los Angeles Times* 21 November 1989, sec. A, p. 25.

12. *San Jose Mercury News* 11 April 1995, sec. B, p. 5.

13. Ibid., 1 May 1995, sec. A, p. 1.

14. *San Francisco Chronicle* 8 January 1995, p. 6/Z3.

15. Ibid., 15 April 1995, sec. A, p. 14.

16. Ibid., 5 June 1987, p. 30.

17. *San Jose Mercury News* 5 June 1987, sec. A, p. 1.

18. Ibid.

19. Ibid.

20. *San Jose Mercury News* 8 November 1994, sec. B, p. 3.

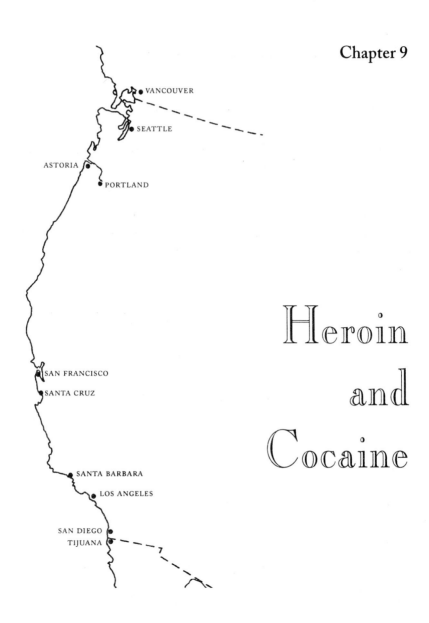

Chapter 9

Heroin and Cocaine

H eroin was first produced by the Bayer Company in Germany in 1898, a year before the first aspirin. It was extracted from morphine, a soluble opium derivative discovered in 1806. Heroin was thought at first to be a therapeutic substitute for opium addiction but was soon found to be four times as powerful and much more addictive than morphine. Its manufacture, a relatively simple extraction process, was banned in the United States in 1924, and even its medical use was prohibited in 1956.[1]

The opium poppies from which heroin is refined flourish in any subtropical climate, often producing two crops per year. Today's principal sources are the highlands of Southeast Asia (Burma, Thailand, and Laos); Southwest Asia (Pakistan, Afghanistan, and Iran); Mexico; and Colombia. Of all these regions, production in Southeast Asia has for some years been the highest.[2]

Heroin use in the United States reached epidemic proportions during and immediately after the Vietnam war, first peaking between 1967 and 1970 and continuing at problematic levels to the present time.[3]

The Indians of Peru and Bolivia have for generations chewed the leaves of the coca plant, *Erythroxylum*, which they found to "clear the mind, elevate mood, and make energy available .... It tones and strengthens the entire digestive tract, probably enhancing the assimilation of foods."[4] By the end of the nineteenth century coca leaves had made their way to Paris and Atlanta, where Parisian winemaker Angelo Mariani produced Vin Mariani, its crucial ingredient being "coca du Perou." Mariani's magic wine received enthusiastic endorsements from such luminaries as Pope Leo XIII and President William McKinley. About the same time, John Styth Pemberton, an Atlanta pharmacist, used coca leaves to spice a popular new temperance drink which he named Coca-Cola. Although the name has survived and flourished, in 1903 the cocaine was removed from Coca-Cola, and by 1914, the extract of the coca leaves had been recognized as a powerful drug and was outlawed in the United States.[5]

Cocaine is extracted in a complex process which begins with soaking coca leaves in water, then using alkali, gasoline, and sulfuric acid to precipitate the alkaloid crystals, which are dried to produce what is called pasta, a brown solid of about one one-hundredth the volume of the coca leaves from which it was extracted. Further refinement produces white crystalline cocaine ready for the market. The quality of the illicit product varies widely. Production of cocaine grew dramatically during the 1970s and 1980s, particularly after 1985, when it was found that a combination of pure cocaine, baking soda, and water produced crack cocaine, cheap, deadly, easy to smoke, and highly addictive.[6]

Such drugs were to become the topic of one particular student's doctoral dissertation, although not in the way one might have expected.

In 1974 Patricia Adler and her husband moved to southern California and became graduate students at the University of California in San Diego (UCSD). Soon after their arrival they met a neighbor named Dave, quiet, friendly, and generous with his cannabis and cocaine. Dave's friends seemed well-to-do, and he was often out of town. When it became clear to the Adlers that he was a wholesale dealer in cocaine and marijuana, Patricia discovered her vocation for the next ten years. From her friendly but persistent questions and close observation of their new circle of friends came a 1984 UCSD doctoral dissertation in sociology and subsequently a book, *Wheeling and Dealing*, now in its second printing. Her book is a uniquely detailed and perceptive description of life in a prosperous community of southern California narcotics dealers.[7]

Adler described these dealers as young, in their twenties and thirties; hedonistic, most having entered the trade to satisfy their own addictions; casual in their handling of large sums of money; and inclined to be overly optimistic about their ability to avoid the legal hazards of drug dealing. Their marijuana and cocaine came, for the most part, from Colombia and was distributed through an economic and social hierarchy based on the scale of each member's operations.

The smugglers' big investments and their shipments of ten to forty kilograms of cocaine, with a market value of more than $10,000 per kilogram, put them at the top of the hierarchy. Wholesale upper-level dealers, like their friend Dave, were next, living comfortably, at somewhat less risk than the smugglers, often dealing in both cocaine and marijuana, and distributing their wares to networks of lower-level dealers. Lower-level dealers in the cocaine trade were called pound dealers, ounce dealers (who generally cut their cocaine with adulterants), and gram dealers, the ultimate street retailers. At each level downward the price per gram more than doubled. The gram dealers, at the bottom of the hierarchy, charged fifty to sixty dollars per half-gram of adulterated cocaine or twenty to twenty-five dollars per "rock," a one-fifth-gram crystal of crack, the standard unit of street sale.[8]

By the late 1980s a major part of the Colombian cocaine smuggled into California was coming through Mexico, rather than directly from Colombia by air or sea. Much of this multibillion-dollar business was eluding the efforts of federal authorities because the contraband was hidden in the large volume of legitimate commerce across the Mexican border.

Then, in the fall of 1989, the Drug Enforcement Administration made a major bust which not only broke up a big smuggling operation but also revealed the tremendous volume of Colombian cocaine coming into California.

Late in the evening of September 28, 1989, acting on a telephone tip from a neighboring business, the DEA and Los Angeles police raided a warehouse in Sylmar, a San Fernando Valley suburb of Los Angeles, in which they found a cache of almost twenty tons of pure cocaine.

102

The drugs were in boxes, piled from floor to ceiling, packed with one-kilogram packages wrapped in burlap. Near them, in cartons and black canvas bags, was $10 million in cash, mostly twenty and hundred-dollar bills. DEA agents estimated the total street value of the seizure at more than $6.7 billion and termed it "the largest in world history." In a heavily armed convoy they transported the money to a Los Angeles bank, and the Los Angeles police department dispatched a SWAT team to Sylmar to guard the cocaine.[9]

The front part of the warehouse, its sign saying "Adriana's," contained a substantial decoy stock of plastic owls, piñatas, and religious paintings on black velvet. Adriana's had been in business for two years at the time of the raid, renting the warehouse for $1,700 per month, paid promptly in twenty-dollar bills. There was a large empty trailer with New Mexico license plates parked beside the loading ramp. The front fifteen feet of the trailer, behind a partition which matched the inside walls, was a concealed storage compartment, presumably used for cocaine. In the warehouse office were records of transactions with both Medellín and Cali cartels, the two principal Colombian drug networks. When DEA agents and Los Angeles police entered the building, there was no one there, and the door was secured with an inexpensive padlock. The neighbors described the tenants of the warehouse as pleasant, well dressed, clean cut, and well mannered. It did occur to these observers that they seemed unusually well-off for dealers in plastic owls, pinatas, and velvet paintings.[10]

The Drug Enforcement Administration identified Mexican national Rafael Muñóz Talavera as head of the organization and shortly raided his 10,000-square-foot villa in El Paso, Texas. Muñóz also owned a fashionable restaurant in El Paso and sixty properties in Mexico, including five ranches and houses in

Acapulco and Cancun. Muñóz and his wife and children had departed for Ciudad Juárez, Mexico, when the news from Sylmar arrived, but six of his colleagues were arrested in southern California. Carlos Tapia-Ponce, Muñóz's senior deputy, and Tapia-Ponce's son Hector were arrested in Las Vegas the following day. Tapia-Ponce's son-in-law, James McTague, was the only U.S. citizen among those apprehended.[11]

At their trial, in September of 1990, DEA agent Palmira López estimated Tapia-Ponce's income at $3 million per day at the time of the raid and said the Sylmar warehouse was the nation's largest cocaine distribution center. López calculated, from Adriana's office records, that within the three months preceding the bust seventy-seven tons of Colombian cocaine had arrived from desert air strips in northern Mexico, transported in big-rig trailers ostensibly loaded with tourist-quality arts, crafts, and pottery products.[12]

Muñóz was arrested in Juárez on November 1, 1989. The DEA tried to have him extradited, since several of his colleagues in the Sylmar warehouse identified him as head of the organization, but he was able to protect himself from extradition. He was tried in Juárez and acquitted on January 17, 1991. He was arrested again in Tijuana on September 20, 1992, and brought to Hermosillo where, on March 20, 1995, with evidence supplied by U.S. agents, he received a twenty-four-year sentence. He appealed, and his sentence was reversed on March 2, 1996, the judge ruling that he had been illegally tried twice for the same offense. In a major report on Muñóz in the *The New York Times*, reporters Sam Dillon and Craig Pyes said that he was housed, during his trials, in comfortable suites in Mexican federal prisons, including one with a bar. They reported in April 1998 that he was in firm control of his organization in Ciudad Juárez, on the border between Mexico and Texas.[13]

By 1992 the volume of Colombian cocaine coming through Mexico had reached a level which caused alarmed federal agents to increase their efforts at interdiction. Although these efforts were not enough to end the flow of cocaine into California, the Sylmar raid interfered enough with shipments by the Medellín cartel, the principal source of the Sylmar cache, to cause smugglers to look for new modes of operation.

One of these experiments was particularly ingenious. On October 26, 1992, Harold Satizabal and Luís Henry Bustos Delgado were arrested in Garden Grove, in northern Orange County, to which they had just brought two dog kennels.

These kennels, identical in appearance to an American product selling for $130, were remarkably enhanced; FBI and DEA agents estimated that they were worth $500,000 each. They were made of a combination of fiber glass and pure cocaine, so fused as to avoid detection. Bustos had picked up a similar container at the airport a year earlier and taken it to a Riverside warehouse where he removed the metal parts, ground it up, and chemically extracted between 4.5 and 7 kilograms of crack-quality cocaine. Unfortunately for the Satizabal and Bustos, the FBI had been alerted, recorded this process with a hidden TV camera, and was prepared for the shipment which arrived in 1992.[14]

A similarly ingenious smuggling scheme was revealed in the June 1988 arrest of Andrew Kit Wong in San Francisco after a collaborative investigation by the DEA, the Hong Kong Police, and the Chinese Ministry of Public Safety turned up a seven-pound heroin shipment concealed in a shipment of goldfish. The heroin was packed in condoms sewn into 140 eviscerated goldfish, which were mixed with a thousand live goldfish in plastic-lined boxes. The goldfish were shipped from Hong Kong to the Goldfish Aquarium, in which Wong was a partner with two other San Francisco men and Tsz Keung Wong, arrested in July in Hong Kong in possession of twenty pounds of heroin. The goldfish ring underestimated the curiosity of Hong Kong inspectors and the cooperative efforts of U.S. and Chinese authorities, which cost Andrew Wong a mandatory ten-year prison sentence and a $12 million fine.[15]

Heroin continued to be very much a part of the smuggling scene. A spectacularly large shipment was seized by customs agents in May 1991 when they found over half a ton of nearly pure heroin aboard a Taiwanese freighter in the port of Oakland. Assistant U.S. Attorney John Kennedy, who prosecuted the case, estimated the value of the 1,080-pound shipment, in wooden crates of small packages wrapped as gifts, to be over a billion dollars.

It was addressed to Jim Juichang Chen of Danville, California, for delivery to a warehouse in nearby Hayward. Customs agents removed most of the heroin, substituting electronic monitoring equipment, and sent the crates on to the warehouse, where on May 20 they arrested Chen, his wife Lucy, his brother Mike Chen, and his sister-in-law, Kelly Chen. Li Yuen Shing, a fifth partner, was apprehended a few days later in Massachusetts. Jim and Lucy Chen faced routine confiscation of their house in the fashionable Blackhawk subdivision in Danville, worth half a million dollars, but they were permitted to deed it to their attorney to cover trial costs.[16]

While the Chens were languishing in jail, another East Bay heroin smuggler, who operated on a more modest scale, though with better luck and what DEA agent Robert Bender described as "a very sophisticated organization," was ending a twenty-month sentence for a fraudulent passport application and returning to his prosperous heroin trade. Pius Ailemen, born in Lagos, Nigeria, in 1964, was one of six children of a wealthy family; his father was onetime Minister of Health and owner of large rubber and cocoa plantations. His oldest brother was reported at the time of the trial to be a prominent Nigerian politician.

In 1981 Pius Ailemen arrived in San Diego. Without passport or visa, he had paid $7,000 to smugglers in Amsterdam and Mexico. He moved to the San Francisco Bay area and shortly acquired a Social Security card, a Louisiana driver's license, and a passport in the name of Muhammed Popoola. He later reported that he worked during this time as a dealer in used hotel furniture, a clothes designer, and an importer of rubber and palm kernels.

He was a successful entrepreneur, attractive, well dressed, and gregarious. He didn't drink or use drugs; he had many friends, many of them beautiful women, prominent politicians, athletes, and entertainers. There was a brief flurry of media interest in early 1994 when it was discovered that he had exchanged telephone calls with Jesse Jackson's sons, Jonathan and Jesse, Jr., who in 1991 had used two of their father's credit cards to help Ailemen buy an Alfa Romeo convertible. However, the Jackson brothers were not further implicated in his drug dealing.[17]

Some time during the early 1980s he discovered that he could readily obtain excellent Asian heroin in Nigeria and that there was a flourishing market for it in American cities. He engaged attractive young women nineteen to twenty-three years of age as couriers, required that they not be drug users, and paid them about $3,000 per trip to Europe or Africa.

One of these young women, who said she had organized other "mules," as drug couriers were called, and made six trips herself, testified that Ailemen had told her she was carrying diamonds. The drugs she carried were in taped packages, concealed under a girdle, over which she wore "loose, baggy clothing." She told

San Francisco Chronicle reporters that "he wanted us to look like well-dressed students on a holiday."[18]

Drug enforcement agents began to suspect Ailemen of heroin smuggling in 1987, tapped his phone, followed his movements and those of his friends, and in October 1988 arrested several of his couriers at Chicago's O'Hare Airport. Apprehensive after his mules' arrest, Ailemen spent several months in Nigeria but eventually returned to Oakland. There, on October 6, 1989, federal agents arrested him and charged him with smuggling heroin and of making false statements on a passport application.[19]

At his trial in February 1990 he testified that in 1987 a friend in Nigeria had asked him to help ship some diamonds to the United States and that he didn't know that his couriers were carrying heroin until their arrest in 1988. During part of his dramatic testimony he cried. To the intense annoyance of U.S. District Judge Samuel Conti, the jury acquitted him of all but the passport perjury charge, for which Judge Conti gave him a maximum five-year sentence and a $10,000 fine. Through the adept efforts of his attorney, Gail Shifman of San Francisco, the fine was reduced to $2,000 and he was paroled from a Louisiana jail in June 1991 after spending a total of twenty months in confinement, and he was soon back in Oakland in the heroin trade.

He rented a twentieth-floor flat in a fashionable apartment complex called Park Bellevue, overlooking Lake Merritt, and reestablished his lines of communication. DEA agent Carl Estelle later testified that in December 1992 he bought an ounce of heroin from Ellis Quarshie, one of Ailemen's dealers, paying $6,000 for it. In February 1993, at Quarshie's house, he bought 100 grams from Ailemen himself, for $21,000. On September 18 DEA agents arrested Dele Ailemen, Pius's brother, as he arrived in the Los Angeles airport and confiscated $48,000 in cash which he was carrying.[20]

Pius Ailemen was not arrested again until December 1993 when two female federal agents, one from the DEA and one from the FBI, listening in a room next to his in the Mayflower Hotel in Washington, heard him screaming and rescued him from two men who were attacking him. One of the assailants was also arrested; one escaped.

Eighteen of Ailemen's co-conspirators were shortly picked up, including his brother Dele, Ellis Quarshie, and Joycelyn Lane, a courier arrested in London with nearly seven pounds of heroin strapped to her body.[21]

A few weeks after Ailemen's arrest in Washington, federal agents routinely confiscated his 1991 Alfa Romeo and $4,900 in cash. This action and an appellate court decision the following summer provided Ailemen's enterprising attorney, Gail Shifman, with the means, at Ailemen's trial in May 1995, of evading most of the charges against him. The previous year, in July 1994, the Ninth Circuit Court of Appeals had ruled that the combination of criminal prosecution and confiscation of drug dealers' property constituted double jeopardy. This decision caused gnashing of teeth in the drug enforcement establishment, for which confiscated drug profits had become a powerful weapon and a generous source of income. The decision was, however, of major relevance to this, Ailemen's second trial.[22]

U.S. Attorney Michael Yamaguchi's carefully built case consisted of forty-three counts of drug smuggling and conspiracy and one count of money laundering. On the recommendation of Magistrate Wayne Brazil, U.S. District Judge Vaughn Walker, with some discomfort, dismissed all smuggling and conspiracy charges against Ailemen and two other defendants. He did, however, sustain the money laundering charge against Ailemen as being unaffected by the double jeopardy decision. Money laundering carries a maximum sentence of twenty years.[23]

The following year, on June 24, 1996, the U.S. Supreme Court reversed the Ninth Circuit Court decision and a similar double jeopardy ruling by the Sixth Circuit Court. The appellate court in San Francisco reinstated forty-one charges which it had previously dismissed and Ailemen's term was extended.[24]

Endnotes

1. George R. Gay and E. Leong Way, "Pharmacology of the Opiate Narcotics," *It's So Good, Don't Even Try in Once: Heroin in Perspective*, ed. David E. Smith and George R. Gay (New York: Prentice-Hall, 1972), pp. 45–58.

2. Leon Gibson Hunt and Carl D. Chambers, *The Heroin Epidemics* (New York: Spectrum Publications, 1976); and Michael Childress, *A System Description of the Heroin Trade* (Santa Monica: Rand Corp., 1993), pp. 8–23.

3. Ibid.

4. David Lee, *Cocaine Handbook; an Essential Reference* (Berkeley: The And/Or Press, 1981), pp. 24–25.

5. Ibid.

6. Paul B. Stares, *Global Habit: the Drug Problem in a Borderless World* (Washington: The Brookings Institution, 1996), pp. 32–33.

7. Patricia A. Adler, *Wheeling and Dealing; an Ethnography of an Upper-Level Drug Dealing and Smuggling Community* (New York: Columbia University Press, 1985).

8. Ibid., 58–59; and *Los Angeles Times* 30 September 1989, p. 24.

9. *Los Angeles Times* 30 September 1989, sec. A, p. 1 ff.

10. Ibid., p. 26.

11. *Los Angeles Times* 7 October 1989, sec. A, p. 1 ff.; 6 November 1989, sec. A, p. 1 ff.; and 24 September 1990, sec. B, p. 1.

12. *Los Angeles Times* 7 October 1989, sec. A, p. 1 ff.; 6 November 1989, sec. A, p. 1 ff.; and 24 September 1990, sec. B, p. 1.

13. *The New York Times* 15 April 1998, sec. A, pp. 1, 14.

14. *Los Angeles Times* 28 October 1992, sec. A, pp. 1, 3.

15. *San Francisco Chronicle* 4 June 1988, sec. A, p. 3; 27 July 1988, sec. A, p. 4; and 30 July 1988, sec. A, p. 2.

16. *San Jose Mercury News* 28 July 1991, sec. B, p. 5.

17. *San Francisco Chronicle* 4 February 1994, sec. A, p. 21.

18. Ibid., 31 December 1993, sec. A, p. 1.

19. Ibid.

20. Ibid.

21. Ibid.

22. *San Francisco Chronicle* 9 May 1995, sec. A, p. 1.

23. Ibid., 10 May 1995, sec. A, p. 17; and *San Jose Mercury News*, 10 May 1995, sec. B, p. 3.

24. *The New York Times* 30 June 1996, sec. E, p. 16; *United States v. Guy Jerome Ursery* and *United States v. $405,089.23 in United States Currency*, 518 Sup. Ct. 267 (1996); and *San Francisco Chronicle* 17 September 1996, sec. A, p. 17.

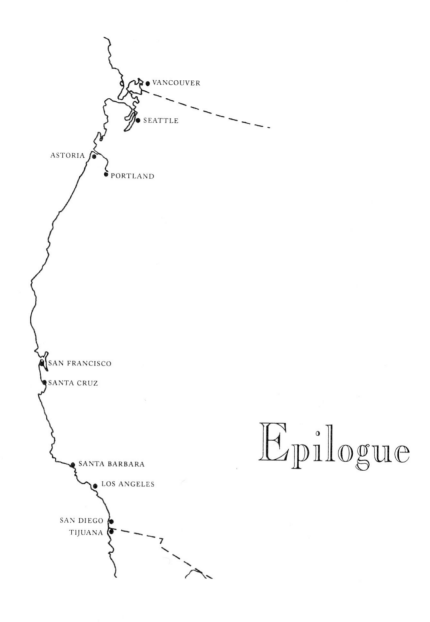

VANCOUVER

SEATTLE

ASTORIA

PORTLAND

SAN FRANCISCO

SANTA CRUZ

SANTA BARBARA

LOS ANGELES

SAN DIEGO
TIJUANA

Epilogue

I n the two centuries since Governor Arrillaga tried in vain to keep Yankee merchantmen from trading Asian silks and European brandy to the padres and ranchers of Alta California in exchange for otter pelts, the West Coast has changed dramatically. Where cattle once grazed, tall glass towers rise out of the smog, its acrid fumes corroding leaves and lungs. The tinkle of cowbells has given way to the roar of freeway traffic, punctuated by an occasional gunshot.

Sailing to the Sandwich Islands in those days took as much as a month; a jet now takes four hours. With its vast new population, the West now has its share of crime, and of that share the heroin of Pius Ailemen and his competitors has been an important part.

And in spite of strenuous efforts to stop them at the border and off the Pacific coast, the coyotes of Sonora and the snakeheads of Fujian continue their commerce in human misery.

In the early nineteenth century, smuggling was more genteel than it is today. Then it was widely accepted, victimless. Now it is deservedly in such disfavor as to earn Calvin Robinson a life sentence without parole; its addict victims number in the millions. The morning news reveals a continuing flood of Colombian cocaine, hundreds of Asian immigrants crammed into rusty freighters, and shipments of endangered animals.

Night landings are still with us.

Bibliography

Adler, Patricia. *Wheeling and Dealing: an Ethnography of an Upper-Level Drug Dealing and Smuggling Community.* New York: Columbia University Press, 1985.

Allen, Everett S. *The Black Ships: Rumrunners of Prohibition.* Boston: Little, Brown & Co., 1979.

Bancroft, Hubert Howe. *The History of California.* 7 vols. San Francisco: The History Company, 1890.

Chapman, Charles E. *A History of California; the Spanish Period.* New York: Macmillan, 1930.

Childress, Michael. *A System Description of the Heroin Trade.* Santa Monica: The Rand Corp., 1993.

Clements, William M. Library. *Eighteenth Century Documents Relating to the Royal Forests, the Sheriffs and Smuggling; Selected from the Shelbourne Manuscripts.* Arthur Lyon Cross, ed. New York: Macmillan, 1928.

Cleveland, H. W. S. *Voyages of a Merchant Navigator of the Days That Are Past.* New York: Harper Brothers, 1886.

Coughlin, Magdalen. "Boston Smugglers on the Coast (1797–1821): an Insight into the American Acquisition of California." *California Historical Society Quarterly* 46 (1967): 99–120.

The Daily Alta California, San Francisco.

Dana, Richard Henry. *Two Years Before the Mast.* 2 vols. Los Angeles: Ward Ritchie Press, 1964.

Davis, Vernon C. *Blood on the Border: Criminal Behavior and Illegal Immigration along the Southern U.S. Border.* New York: Vantage Press, 1991.

Davis, William Heath. *Seventy-Five Years in California.* San Francisco: John Howell Books, 1929.

Hammond, George P., ed. *The Larkin Papers: Personal, Business, and Official Correspondence of Thomas Oliver Larkin.* 10 vols. Berkeley: University of California Press, 1951–64.

Hunt, Leon Gibson and Carl D. Chambers. *The Heroin Epidemics.* New York: Spectrum Publication, 1976.

Hyman, Frank J. *Historic Writings: a Recording of Facts and Descriptions Covering the Area on the Mendocino Coast in and around Fort Bragg.* N.p., 1966.

Jenkins, John A. *Ladies' Man; the Life and Trials of Marvin Mitchelson.* New York: St. Martin's Press, 1992.

Kane, Harry H. *Opium Smoking in America and China.* New York: G. P. Putnam's Sons, 1882.

Krout, John Allen. *The Origins of Prohibition.* New York: Russell & Russell, 1966.

Kyvig, David E., ed. *Law, Alcohol, and Order: Perspectives on National Prohibition.* Contributions in American History, no. 110. Westport, CT: Greenwood Press, 1985.

Lee, David. *Cocaine Handbook: an Essential Reference.* Berkeley: The And/Or Press, 1981.

Los Angeles Times.

Lummis, Charles F. "Mr. Eayrs of Boston." *Out West* 30 (1909): 159–166.

Lydon, Sandy. *Chinese Gold: the Chinese in the Monterey Bay Region.* Capitola, CA: The Capitola Book Company, 1984.

McCoy, Alfred W. *The Politics of Heroin.* Brooklyn, NY: Lawrence Hill Books, 1991.

The New York Times.

Noble, William. *Bookbanning in America.* Middlebury, VT: Paul S. Eriksson, 1990.

Ogden, Adele. *The California Sea Otter Trade, 1784–1848.* Berkeley: University of California Press, 1941.

"The Opium Trade." *Living Age* 35 (1852): 546–552.

Prince, Carl E. and Mollie Keller. *The United States Customs Service: a Bicentennial History.* Washington: Government Printing Office, 1989.

"Report of Reference Committee on Legislation." *Journal of the American Medical Association* 68 (1917): 1837.

Richman, Irving Berdine. *California Under Spain and Mexico, 1535–1847.* Boston: Houghton Mifflin, 1965.

San Francisco Call.

San Francisco Chronicle.

San Francisco Examiner.

San Jose Mercury News.

Santa Cruz Evening News.

Santa Cruz Sentinel.

Santa Cruz Surf.

Scammon, C. M. "Sea Otters." *Overland Monthly* 4 (January 1870): 25–30.

Sinclair, Andrew. *Prohibition: the Era of Excess.* Boston: Little, Brown & Co., 1962.

Smith, Adam. *An Inquiry into the Nature and Causes of the Wealth of Nations.* Oxford: The Clarendon Press, 1976.

Smith, David E. and George R. Gay, eds. *It's So Good Don't Even Try It Once: Heroin in Perspective.* New York: Prentice-Hall, 1972.

Smith, Page. *America Enters the World.* New York: McGraw-Hill, 1985.

Stagnaro, Malio J. "Malio J. Stagnaro, the Santa Cruz Genovese." Interview by Elizabeth Spedding Calciano. Manuscript. 1975. McHenry Library Special Collections, University of California, Santa Cruz.

Stares, Paul B. *Global Habit: the Drug Problem in a Borderless World.* Washington, D.C.: The Brookings Institution, 1996.

U.S. Coast Guard. Monterey Group. Unclassified dispatches, received 2 and 3 June 1993.

The Washington Post.

Watsonville Register-Pajaronian.

Willoughby, Malcolm F. *Rum War at Sea.* Washington, D.C.: U.S. Coast Guard, 1964.

Index

Hellgate Press

Hellgate Press is named after the historic and rugged Hellgate Canyon on southern Oregon's scenic Rogue River. The raging river that flows below the canyon's towering jagged cliffs has always attracted a special sort of individual — someone who seeks adventure. From the pioneers who bravely pursued the lush valleys beyond, to the anglers and rafters who take on its roaring challenges today — Hellgate Press publishes books that personify this adventurous spirit. Our books are about military history, adventure travel, and outdoor recreation. On the following pages, we would like to introduce you to some of our latest titles and encourage you to join in the celebration of this unique spirit.

Our books are in your favorite bookstore or you can order them direct at **1-800-228-2275** *or visit our Website at http://www.psi-research.com/hellgate.htm*

ARMY MUSEUMS
West of the Mississippi
by Fred L. Bell, SFC Retired

ISBN: 1-55571-395-5
Paperback: $17.95

A guide book for travelers to the army museums of the west, as well as a source of information about the history of the site where the museum is located. Contains detailed information about the contents of the museum and interesting information about famous soldiers stationed at the location or specific events associated with the facility. These twenty-three museums are in forts and military reservations which represent the colorful heritage in the settling of the American West.

BYRON'S WAR
I Never Will Be Young Again...
by Byron Lane

ISBN: 1-55571-402-1
Hardcover: $21.95

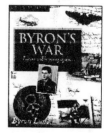

Based on letters that were mailed home and a personal journal written more than fifty years ago during World War II, Byron's War brings the war life through the eyes of a very young air crew officer. It depicts how the life of this young American changed through cadet training, the experiences as a crew member flying across the North Atlantic under wartime hazards to the awesome responsibility assigned to a nineteen year-old when leading hundreds of men and aircraft where success or failure could seriously impact the outcome of the war.

GULF WAR DEBRIEFING BOOK

An After Action Report ISBN: 1-55571-396-3
by Andrew Leyden Paperback: $18.95

Whereas most books on the Persian Gulf War tell an "inside story" based on someone else's opinion, this book lets you draw your own conclusions about the war by providing you with a meticulous review of events and documentation all at your fingertips. Includes lists of all military units deployed, a detailed account of the primary weapons used during the war, and a look at the people and politics behind the military maneuvering.

FROM HIROSHIMA WITH LOVE

ISBN: 1-55571-404-8
by Raymond A. Higgins Paperback: $18.95

This remarkable story is written from actual detailed notes and diary entries kept by Lieutenant Commander Wallace Higgins. Because of his industrial experience back in the United States and with the reserve commission in the Navy, he was an excellent choice for military governor of Hiroshima. Higgins was responsible for helping rebuild a ravaged nation of war. He developed an unforeseen respect for the Japanese, the culture, and one special woman.

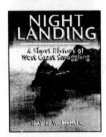

NIGHT LANDING

A Short History of West Coast Smuggling ISBN: 1-55571-449-8
by David W. Heron Paperback: $13.95

Night Landing reveals the true stories of smuggling off the shores of California from the early 1800s to the present. It is a provocative account of the many attempts to illegally trade items such as freon, drugs, sea otters, and diamonds. This unusual chronicle also profiles each of these ingenious, but over-optimistic criminals and their eventual apprehension.

ORDER OF BATTLE

Allied Ground Forces of Operation Desert Storm ISBN: 1-55571-493-5
by Thomas D. Dinackus Paperback: $17.95

Based on extensive research, and containing information not previously available to the public, *Order of Battle: Allied Ground Forces of Operation Desert Storm*, is a detailed study of the Allied ground combat units that served in Operation Desert Storm. In addition to showing unit assignments, it includes the insignia and equipment used by the various units in one of the largest military operations since the end of WWII.

PILOTS, MAN YOUR PLANES!

A History of Naval Aviation ISBN: 1-55571- 466-8
by Wilbur H. Morrison Hardbound: $ 33.95

An account of naval aviation from Kitty Hawk to the Gulf War, *Pilots, Man Your Planes!* tells the story of naval air growth from a time when planes were launched from battleships to the major strategic element of naval warfare it is today. Full of detailed maps and photographs. Great for anyone with an interest in aviation.

REBIRTH OF FREEDOM

From Nazis and Communists to a New Life in America ISBN: 1-55571-492-7
by Michael Sumichrast   Paperback: $ 16.95

"...a fascinating account of how the skill, ingenuity and work ethics of an individual, when freed from the yoke of tyranny and oppression, can make a lasting contribution to Western society. Michael Sumichrast's autobiography tells of his first loss of freedom to the Nazis, only to have his native country subjected to the tyranny of the Communists. He shares his experiences of life in a manner that makes us Americans, and others, thankful to live in a country where individual freedom is protected."

— *General Alexander M. Haig, Former Secretary of State*

THE WAR THAT WOULD NOT END

U.S. Marines in Vietnam, 1971-1973   ISBN: 1-55571-420-X
by Major Charles D. Melson, USMC (Ret)   Paperback: $19.95

When South Vietnamese troops proved unable to "take over" the war from their American counterparts, the Marines had to resume responsibility. Covering the period 1971-1973, Major Charles D. Melson, who served in Vietnam, describes all the strategies, battles, and units that broke a huge 1972 enemy offensive. The book contains a detailed look at this often ignored period of America's longest war.

WORDS OF WAR

From Antiquity to Modern Times   ISBN: 1-55571-491-9
by Gerald Weland   Paperback: $ 13.95

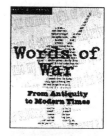

Words of War is a delightful romp through military history. Lively writing leads the reader to an under- standing of a number of soldierly quotes. The result of years of haunting dusty dungeons in libraries, obscure journals and microfilm files, this unique approach promises to inspire many casual readers to delve further into the circumstances surrounding the birth of many quoted words.

WORLD TRAVEL GUIDE

A Resource for Travel and Information   ISBN: 1-55571- 494-3
by Barry Mowell   Paperback: $ 19.95

The resource for the modern traveler, *World Travel Guide: A Resource for Travel and Information* is both informative and enlightening. It contains maps, social and economic information, concise information concerning entry requirements, availability of healthcare, transportation and crime. Numerous Website and embassy listings are provided for additional free information. A one-page summary contains general references to the history, culture and other characteristics of interest to the traveler or those needing a reference atlas.

TO ORDER OR FOR MORE INFORMATION
CALL 1·800·228·2275

K-9 SOLDIERS

Vietnam and After   ISBN: 1-55571-495-1
by Paul B. Morgan   Paperback: $13.95

A retired US Army officer, former Green Beret, Customs K-9 and Security Specialist, Paul B. Morgan has written *K-9 Soldiers*. In his book, Morgan relates twenty-four brave stories from his lifetime of working with man's best friend in combat and on the streets. They are the stories of dogs and their handlers who work behind the scenes when a disaster strikes, a child is lost or some bad guy tries to outrun the cops.

AFTER THE STORM

A Vietnam Veteran's Reflection   ISBN: 1-55571-500-1
by Paul Drew   Paperback: $14.95

Even after twenty-five years, the scars of the Vietnam War are still felt by those who were involved. *After the Storm: A Vietnam Veteran's Reflection* is more than a war story. Although it contains episodes of combat, it does not dwell on them. It concerns itself more on the mood of the nation during the war years, and covers the author's intellectual and psychological evolution as he questions the political and military decisions that resulted in nearly 60,000 American deaths.

GREEN HELL

The Battle for Guadalcanal   ISBN: 1-55571-498-6
by William J. Owens   Paperback: $18.95

This is the story of thousands of Melanesian, Australian, New Zealand, Japanese, and American men who fought for a poor insignificant island is a faraway corner of the South Pacific Ocean. For the men who participated, the real battle was of man against jungle. This is the account of land, sea and air units covering the entire six-month battle. Stories of ordinary privates and seamen, admirals and generals who survive to claim the victory that was the turning point of the Pacific War.

OH, WHAT A LOVELY WAR

                                                   ISBN: 1-55571-502-8
by Evelyn A. Luscher   Paperback: $14.95

This book tells you what history books do not. It is war with a human face. It is the unforgettable memoir of British soldier Gunner Stanley Swift through five years of war. Intensely personal and moving, it documents the innermost thoughts and feelings of a young man as he moves from civilian to battle-hardened warrior under the duress of fire.

THROUGH MY EYES

91st Infantry Division, Italian Campaign 1942-1945   ISBN: 1-55571-497-8
by Leon Weckstein   Paperback: $14.95

Through My Eyes is the true account of an Average Joe's infantry days before, during and shortly after the furiously fought battle for Italy. The author's front row seat allows him to report the shocking account of casualties and the rest-time shenanigans during the six weeks of the occupation of the city of Trieste. He also recounts in detail his personal roll in saving the historic Leaning Tower of Pisa.

Order Directly From Hellgate Press

You can purchase any of these Hellgate Press titles directly by sending us this completed order form.

Hellgate Press

P.O. Box 3727
Central Point, OR 97502

To order call, 1-800-228-2275
Fax 1-541-476-1479

For inquiries and international orders,
call 1-541-479-9464

TITLE	PRICE	QUANTITY	COST
Army Museums: West of the Mississippi	$13.95		
Byron's War	$21.95		
From Hiroshima With Love	$18.95		
Gulf War Debriefing Book	$18.95		
Night Landing	$13.95		
Order of Battle	$17.95		
Pilots, Man Your Planes!	$33.95		
Rebirth of Freedom	$16.95		
The War That Would Not End	$19.95		
Words of War	$13.95		
World Travel Guide	$19.95		
Memories Series			
K-9 Soldiers	$13.95		
After The Storm	$14.95		
Green Hell	$18.95		
Oh, What A Lovely War!	$14.95		
Through My Eyes	$14.95		

If your purchase is:	your shipping is:		
up to $25	$5.00	**Subtotal**	$
$25.01–$50.00	$6.00	**Shipping**	$
$50.01–$100	$7.00	**Grand Total**	$
$100.01–$175	$9.00		
over $175	call		

Thank You For Your Order!

Shipping Information

Name:

Address:

City, State, Zip:

Daytime Phone: Email:

Ship To: (If Different Than Above)

Name:

Address:

City, State, Zip

Daytime Phone:

Payment Method:

For rush orders, Canadian and overseas orders please call for details at (541) 479-9464

☐ Check   ☐ American Express ☐ MasterCard ☐ Visa

Card Number: Expiration Date:

Signature: Exact Name on Card:

For more adventure and military history information visit our Website

Hellgate Press Online

http://www.psi-research.com/hellgate.htm

With information about our latest titles, as well as links to related subject matter.

Hellgate Press Reader Survey

Did you enjoy this Hellgate Press title?
☐ Yes   ☐ No
If no, how would you improve it:

_____
_____
_____

Would you be interested in other titles from Hellgate Press?
☐ Yes   ☐ No

How do you feel about the price?
☐ Too high   ☐ Fair   ☐ Lower than expected

Where did you purchase this book?
☐ Bookstore
☐ Online (Internet)
☐ Catalog
☐ Association/Club
☐ It was a gift
☐ Other: _____

Do you use a personal computer?
☐ Yes   ☐ No

Have you ever purchased anything on the Internet?
☐ Yes   ☐ No

Do you use a personal computer?
☐ Yes   ☐ No

Would you like to receive a Hellgate catalog?
☐ Yes   ☐ No
If yes, please fill out the information below:

**Night Landing
A Short History of
West Coast Smuggling**

Please send this survey to:
PSI Research
c/o Hellgate Press
P.O. Box 3727
Central Point, OR 97526

or fax it: (541) 476-1479
or email your responses to:
info@psi-research.com

Thank You!

Name: _____

Address: _____

City, State, Zip: _____

Email Address (optional): _____